COVID PANDEMIC CRISES

CONVERGENCE INOVATION IN THE DIGITAL ERA

DR. MUKTA GOYAL MR.KRITTIBAAS DATTA

ISBN 979-888606012-6

Dedicated to our Parents, Family, Friends, and Teachers without whom this book Publication would not have been possible.

Contents

Preface

When Covid-19 struck, it compelled societal changes all over the world. Nearly overnight, governments issued orders restricting large crowds, limiting in-person business operations, and encouraging people to work from home as much as possible. As a result, businesses and schools alike began to look for ways to operate remotely, thanks to the internet. They used various collaboration platforms and video conferencing capabilities to stay in touch with colleagues, clients, and students while working from home offices.

To combat the COVID-19 pandemic, WHO has received overwhelming pro-bono assistance from technology companies? 30 of the world's leading digital technology experts convened in a virtual roundtable on April 2 to help advance WHO's collaborative response to COVID-19.

This pandemic has created an unprecedented demand for digital health technology solutions, revealing successful solutions such as population screening, infection tracking, prioritising resource use and allocation, and designing targeted responses.

In different parts of the world, the educational system is facing some of its biggest trials yet, from the COVID-19 pandemic. The continuous closing of Schools and Colleges has vibrated the entire education system.

However, the ability of digital technologies to go beyond that has recently been revealed to the general public. Emerging technologies such as Artificial Intelligence (AI) aid in the development of vaccines, predicting which public health measures will be most effective, and keeping the public informed of scientific developments. They have also enabled us to move much of our lives online, keeping economic and educational systems running when most people are at home and keeping us connected to one another.

However, not all regions and social groups are equally capable of harnessing the power of digital technologies to combat the virus. This book focuses on how the pandemic serves as a widespread test case for the efficacy of these digital solutions, many of which will become permanent fixtures and cause long-term changes in many organisations. The innovations born of necessity may become long-lasting pillars of the organisations, allowing them to thrive long after the pandemic has passed. The coronavirus is forever changing the way we live and work. Some of the behaviours that emerged during the crisis, such as widespread digital adoption, will outlast the pandemic, long after restrictions on activity are lifted. Organizations must respond to these behavioural changes and meet emerging customer demands in order to remain competitive.

This Volume is possible with the blessing of our parents and family members whose continues inspiration guided us for publications this book in time. Our sincere thanks to all the chapter contributors without their contributions this edited volume would not have been possible. As a whole the book got the complete shape because of the great initiative of Notion press. Finally, we do hereby declare that the chapter contributed by the contributors are of their own views; if any discrepancies or legal issues arise out of this publication the contributors will be responsible for this; the editors or publishers will not bear the responsibility.

Dr. Mukta Goyal
Mr.Krittibas Datta

Abstract And Keywords

A study on the Impact on Self Help Groups during and Post Covid 19

Abstract

There are many kinds of disasters in this world. Some are like an earthquake, tsunami, flood, rainfall, etc. in the same kind disease are also one kind of disaster from last many days it affects very badly on all over the world so it is called a disaster. There is one kind of record there is a disease after every 100 years. Like in the 1820 Cholera pandemic, in 1920 Spanish flu, and now in 2020, it's COVID-19. COVID-19: Coronavirus disease 2019. Coronavirus is a single standard RNA virus with a diameter ranging from80-120 nanometers. The first Covid-19 virus was reported in Wuhan, China in December 2019.

from that time this virus is rapidly spread all over the world. It was categorized as a pandemic by WHO(World Health Organization) Covid-19 apart from becoming the greatest threat to global public health of the century is being considered as the largest disrupted in social and economic achievement. This paper brings the suffering of Self Help Groups during the pandemic and its challenges. It primarily focuses on the various aspects of the economic and financial impact that occur due to the outbreak of COVID-19.

Keywords

Self Help Group, Economic Impact, Financial Impact, Pandemic, Digital Marketing.

An analysis of the "Make in India" program and its prospect

Abstract

India has launched the "Make in India" initiative to promote domestic manufacturing. Multinational corporations can produce goods in India. This program was unveiled on September 25, 2014, as the most critical state strategy for direct investment by other nations globally. As a result, India has earned $ 413 billion in investment up to now. Twenty-five brochures and a web portal have been distributed during the project. Foreign capital regulations in different industries had been loosened before the legislation's introduction. Along with this, India's most detailed project, the online portal, was also launched.

Outcomes of COVID 19 featured by students of School Education System in Punjab Province

Abstract

W.H.O. declared Corona a global pandemic on March 11, 2020. The government of Pakistan also imposed lockdown in pursuance of WHO guidelines like other countries which created an emergency situation. This nationwide lockdown to reduce the chances of COVID- 19 infection had created many problems not only financially, but also according to health. This time period has increased mental health problems such as anxiety, depression, changes in behavior, the effectiveness of classes and mental ability to concentrate etc. In addition to them, there was a great fear of getting a Corona infection. The study was conducted on Pakistani students from a public school of Punjab school education department to guess the regular constriction of mental and physical burden on students during this lockdown. We performed this study using a questionnaire to assess the effects faced by the students throughout this whole time span of a pandemic. It was found that female students had a greater impact rather than male students. According to our work mental health, financial difficulties, and behavioral changes were the most common apprehensions of most of the students. We must need considerable efforts to maintain balanced finances, mental health, and behavior in the life of students.

Keywords: COVID- 19, Depression, anxiety, effect, health, Punjab

Online Teacher Education Programme For Higher Education School System To Present Situation Of Covid-19 Pandemic Period

Abstract

The whole education system from elementary to casually live in has been collapsed during the lockdown period of the novel coronavirus disease 2019 not only in India but across Google, the effect of information technology on human life is used and its role in education to cannot be successive it the current scenario of the covid-19 pandemic the contribution of information technology has gained momentum due to closure of educational institutions that rises challenge for student learning.

Keywords: Teacher programme, covid-19, Higher Education, E-learning.

Changing Attitudes Among Teenagers During And After Covid-19: An Analytical Study

Abstract

As coronavirus disease 2019 (COVID19) spreads around the globe, it is also essential to comprehend human psychology as variables connected with pandemic behavior. This perspective is particularly significant for adolescent studies that are unlikely to show rigorous symptoms but have a say in the widening of the virus. COVID19 Investigation of psychological factors related to adolescent behavior during a pandemic. This "self-reported survey", conducted in March 2020 recruited a sample of population-based youth via social Networking sites to participate in a nameless survey. Applicants were qualified if they had internet access, resided in the US, between the range of 13 to18 years old. The findings included surveillance of COVID19 news, social distance, disinfection, and hoarding of actions for seven days, it was declared as a national emergency in the US. Psychological factors included the severity of COVID19, the values of social accountability, social confidence, and attitudes towards self-centeredness. The prior hypothesis is that greater attitudes towards the ruthlessness of COVID19, higher level of social responsibility, and as well as social confidence are connected with better news surveillance, social distance, disinfection, and greater self-interest. It was related to more stockings. The results of this study may emphasize the seriousness of COVID19 and the social impact of pandemic-related behaviours for young people, especially those who do not follow prophylactic health behaviours or engage in the stocking.

Keywords: Changing Attitude, Teenagers, Covid 19, Health, Deaths, Suicidal Attempts, Mental Stress.

"2020:Covid–19 Hits The Education System"

Abstract

In Secondary educational institutions in India are generally based only on age-old traditional methods of teaching-learning, that is, lectures in a face-to-face mode in a classroom. Though some academic units have started following blended learning, still a lot of them are engaged with old methods of teaching. The sudden outbreak of a deadly disease called Covid-19 caused by a Corona Virus (SARS-CoV-2) shook the utmost world. The World Health Organization declared this as a pandemic. This transformed situation challenged the whole education system across the world and forced the educators to shift to an online mode of teaching overnight. Most of the educational institutions that were earlier stubborn to stick only on the traditional pedagogical approach had no option but to shift entirely to online teaching-learning. In this paper the researcher tries to emphasis the importance of Online learning in during and Post –Covid days and made a prominent SWOC analysis of Online Education to understand the whole scenario.

Key Words : - Online Learning, Covid-19, Classroom, SWOC Analysis.

COVID-19 Vaccine Diplomacy in the Indo-Pacific Region

Abstract

India is considered the world's vaccine manufacturing hub which contributes 60 percent to the global vaccine supply. The country has the potential to produce three billion coronavirus disease 2019 (Covid-19) vaccine doses annually. India exported Excel to more than 90 countries received foreign aid from more than 25 countries. India and other countries around the world continue to fight the covid-19 epidemic. On 19 April 2021, the Press Information Bureau released details of India's immunization strategy. The National Expert Group on Vaccine Administration for Covid-19, chaired by Policy Commission member dr. BK Pal was instrumental in developing the strategy. The first large consignment of millions of doses of the Sputnik 'V vaccine from Russia's Serum Institute and India Biotech is set to arrive in India in May 2021. The second wave of the coronavirus and its tragic consequences have persuaded India to accept foreign aid at intervals of 17 years. It has also had a far-reaching strategic impact on India. As a direct result of the epidemic, India's claim to regional supremacy and leadership could take a big hit. These will affect the content and conduct of India's foreign policy in the years to come.

Keywords: Indian foreign policy, covid-19, covaxin, sputnik v, coronavirus.

School Students Academic Stress And Anxiety In The Covid-19 Vaccination

Abstract

The novel coronavirus disease COVID-19 has been declared by the World Health Organization as an international public health emergency and countries all over the world, implemented nationwide lockdowns with the hope of flattening the epidemic curve. Around the world, this has led to the closure of k-12 schools in over 150 countries including India affecting the education of nearly 1billion children (Sahu, 2020) and most of the educational institutions including k-12 schools and colleges remain closed without a clear view regarding their re-opening. The present study focuses on the academic stress and anxiety issues among k-12 school students. Anxiety and stress are highly prevalent among k-12 school students even in normal circumstances, and in India during the covid-19 pandemic, all students encountered fear of infection, exams, challenges of online education, etc. The objective of this study was to assess levels of stress and anxiety and ways of coping among k-12 school students in India by taking the vaccination.

Keywords: k-12, school students, stress, anxiety, covid-19, pandemic, vaccination

Post-Covid Challenges And Coping Strategies For Retail Industry In India: An Empirical Study

Abstract

If one looks at the pandemic caused by the Corona Virus from a broader perspective of changing the global attitude towards a sustainable habit. It raises questions about the potential for universal education under circumstances of worldwide division and rivalry, including knowledge from others, altering community sphere control, and questions about nationwide civilizing practice enhancement. In addition, the accumulation of geographical conditions, technical means, ignorance domination, the emergence of hotspots, and lockdown conditions. With a number of introductory suggestions on how persistent pandemics add to long-term changes in individual attitudes and behaviours in the direction of the surroundings and technology-driven existing environments. The changing scenarios of Indian consumers are demonstrating potential opportunities in the retail industry. SWOT and its subheadings take one to the centre of analysis in the retail industry. From now on, we have formulated a future outlook. The main lifesaver of Indian retail is advertising and promotional strategies. It convinces consumers and comes up with innovative ways to keep them happy. Retail FDI is a controversial issue and can face resistance given the perceived political scenarios. FDI is a decisive moment for Indian retailers, and a final brief explanation of how government policy is affecting retailers.

Keywords: Corona Virus, Post Covid-19, Pandemic, Digital Society, Sustainable Life.

Covid-19 Variants: Alpha Beta Delta And Omicron

Abstract

Just as the second wave of the corona has affected millions of Indians, it has shaken the country's healthcare system. Lockdown conditions in many places have eased somewhat as the number of covid-19, patients has been steadily declining. But doctors are still worried about many of covid-19 new symptoms. The virus SARS-COV-2 upgrade with new variants.

Keywords: Variant, Alpha, Beta, Gama, Delta, Omicron.

CHAPTER ONE

A study on the Impact on Self Help Groups during and Post Covid 19

*-----*Mr. Sajith Kumar B**Prof. Thimmaiah Bayavanda Chinnappa***Mrs. Sajina T Mohan*

Introduction

Self Help Group (SHG) is an informal association of the people who choose to come together to find ways to improve their living conditions. The origin of Self Help Group(SHG) can be traced is from 'Grameen Bank Of Bangladesh'. Which was founded by Mohamad Yunus. Self Help Group (SHG) are an informed association of people who choose to come together to find ways to improve their living conditions. It can be defined as a self-governed peer controlled information group of people with similar socio-economic backgrounds and having a desire to collectively perform a common purpose. Villages face numerous problems related to poverty, illiteracy, lack of skills, lack of formal credit etc. These problems cannot be tackled at an individual level and need collective efforts.

Thus, SHG can become the vehicle of change for the poor and marginalized. SHG relies on the notion of "Self Help" to encourage self-employment and poverty formed in 1975. In NABARD notion of initiated in 1986-1987. The absence of institutional credit available in rural area has led to the establishment of SHGs. The concept of Self Help Group involved organizing the rural poor to meet their production and consumption needs out of their savings. A Self Help Group is a small economically homogeneous affinity group of the rural poor voluntarily coming together to save a small amount regularly. Which are deposited in common funds to meet member emergency needs and to provide collaterals fees, loans decide by the groups.

Review of Literature

India is our country which is known for its population, culture, location etc. second highest population is living in our country, there are many types of communities in that and everyone is trys to earn for living self Help Group is also one kind platform of earning. 40% of Indian women are connected with this platform by which they are living very happily and proudly but this pandemic destroyed many things.

But by the way of the online platform, government vivid schemes every group members are trying to overcome on this.

Objectives of the Study

1. To study the economic impact of Covid-19 on the Self Help Groups in India.
2. To find out the problems faced by Self Help Groups during the lockdown of Covid-19.

Research Methodology

The present research paper "Covid-19 and Self Help Groups" is based on exploratory nature and the entire information are collected from secondary sources. Secondary data is collected through references books, journals, periodicals, online and offline published materials related to Covid-19, and a research paper on Self Help Groups. In addition to collecting some information through formal discussion with members of Self Help Groups.

Economic Impacts

Just like most other disasters in the world, the Coronavirus pandemic too has had a differential impact on men and women. The 2014 Ebola virus and the 2015 Zika virus outbreaks have also proved that women are more vulnerable than men in various ways, which reinforced the persisting gender inequity concerns, especially for the developing world.

At a time when supply chain disruptions in medical products have largely hindered women's menstrual and reproductive health in India, they have been the majority amongst the Covid-19 warriors across the world. 70% of the world's healthcare and social workers are women. In India, estimates show that qualified female healthcare workers account for almost half of the country's health force and are among the more vulnerable groups—women account for a staggering 88.8% of trained nurses and midwives.

According to reports in April, about 20,000 SHGs produced over 19 million masks and 100,000 liters of sanitizers all over India. Since the production is decentralized, these items have been delivered to the masses without having to undergo the logistics of transportation. SHGs have also initiated work related to the provision of rations or cooked food to poor and vulnerable families using the Vulnerability Reduction Fund or with support from state governments and the local administration.

Covid-19 changed the entire world, more specifically the Self-Help Group Bank Linkage Programme (SHG-BLP). It is a landmark model initiated by the National Bank for Agriculture and Rural Development (NABARD) in 1992 to deliver affordable doorstep banking services as part of financial inclusion drive in India. Today, the SHG-BLP is regarded as the largest microfinance programme in the world with a total membership of 100.14 lakhs groups (covering nearly 12 crore households) across India and having extended collateral-free loans of Rs. 87,098 crore to 50.77 lakhs SHGs as of March 31, 2019. It is interesting to note that more than 90 percent of the SHG members are women.

The footprints by the SHGs as community warriors against Covid-19 can be felt across various Indian states. For example, in Tamil Nadu, each PDS shop has been stationed with two SHG volunteers to ensure that people in the queue maintain adequate distance. In Odisha, rural women organised in these SHGs produced more than 1 million cotton masks for police personnel and healthcare workers.

These SHGs have contributed in holistically addressing economic and social needs that have emerged at the community level during the Covid-19 outbreak. The SHGs have consolidated their efforts to work on issues like social distancing, use of masks, quarantine, and psycho-social issues of migrants, care of the elderly population, mental health, and wellbeing, amongst others. Women in these SHGs are creating awareness in the local communities by means such as telephone calls, wall writings, pamphlets, social media, etc.

In Kerala, an SHG named Kudumbashree is helping dispel fake news through its network of Whats App groups with more than 100,000 women as members. These platforms are specifically leveraged to disseminate urgent and authentic information regarding the pandemic. It is also involved in running 1,300 kitchens across Kerala and are providing food to those who are bedridden or under quarantine. The Mahila Arthik Vikas Mahamandal (MAVIM) and the numerous women SHGs operating under it played a crucial role in combating the socio-economic impact of the pandemic in rural Maharashtra. These women even contributed approximately 11 lakhs to the Chief Minister's Relief Fund through a MAVIM-driven donation campaign.

Problems

There are various kinds of challenges faced by the members Self Help Groups during the Covid-19 lockdown, but in this challenges they got various kinds of opportunities like-

1. **Updating members about meetings, transactions, and work:**
2. Due to lockdown there is issue of giving updates about group's work to the group members if they are living very far away from each others. It is quite difficult to inform the members about the timeing of work and all.
3. **Conducting physical meetings:**
4. If group members are living in Covid-19 red zone area then it is very risky to take a any kind of physical meetings.
5. **Depositing currency notes in the group members:**
6. Due to lockdown many group member's earnings is down then there is a issue of depositing currency.
7. **Mobilizing savings throughout the group members:**
8. Due to less depositing there is a problem of savings.
9. **Making the group members user friendly for online transactions:**
10. If group members are not using digital platform for transactions then there is a challenge to the head of the group to make the member user friendly for online transactions.
11. **Mainating the records of the transactions:**
12. This is another kind of challenge to the group members to maintain the record of the group. Because of above-maintained problems.
13. **Update the members for online selling:**
14. Update the members for the online selling means sell their products by using a various online platforms like Amazon, Flipcard, Meeshoo, and Myntra, etc.

Opportunities

Most of the SHGs meet physically. The Ministry of Rural Development recommended that SHG members follow physical distancing guidelines, which may continue after the lockdown, limiting the ability of women's group members to meet. The regular meetings were stopped. Therefore the groups had some kinds of opportunities like

1. **To use digital platform for product sell:** Groups are uses digital media like WhatsApp, Facebook, Instagram etc. for their selling
2. **To use internet media for online transactions:** Group members are now able to use to online banking for their transactions.
3. **To expand their area of selling:** Self-help groups are now selling their products to a vast areas like districts, states, the whole countries by the way of online media.
4. **To change their production:** Self-help groups are now producing demand-based products like masks, sanitizers, PPE Kits and face shields etc. Groups are not only produced this but also sells also these types of products.
5. **Use of new government schemes:** Self-help groups are now using new schemes given by governments after pandemics. A scheme like PMFEME-Prime Minister Formalisation of Micro Food Processing Enterprises, Atmanirbhar Bharat.
6. **Launching new scheme for sell:** Self-help groups are now implementing new schemes for cell growth, production growth like giving offers like discounts, sell, buy one get one, etc.

Conclusion

This pandemic Covid-19 affected very much on various fields. Self Help Groups also get impacted very badly because of pandemic lockdown like their products remains unsealed, due to unsell they are selling at a lower rate to return their loans. Group member's contacts became less that also impacted not only their productions but also their sellings.

Now they changed their production they are producing and selling demand-based products like masks, sanitizers, PPE Kits, etc. They are using digital media for their selling like they are using Amazone, Flipkart, WhatsApp, Facebook, etc. for selling. Because of this their area of selling and working is expanded. Also, they are using online banking for transactions which is a good sign of the country's development.

References

1. www.wikipedia.com
2. www.researchgate.com

3. www.shodhganga.com
4. www.google.com
5. http://www.worldbank.org/en/news/feature/2020/04/11/women-self-help-groups-combact-covid-19-corona-virus-pandemic-india
6. http://www.thehindubusinessline.com/opinion/how-self-groups-can-sustain-during-covid/article31557348.ece
7. http://www.worldbank.org

CHAPTER TWO

Use of Social Media: An Innovation during the Covid 19 --* Krittibas Datta

-----**_*Krittibas Datta_**

Introduction: In modern times social media is an internet-based form of communication. Social media platforms allow users to have conversations, share information, and create web content. There are many forms of social media, including blogs, micro-blogs, wikis, social networking sites, photo-sharing sites, instant messaging, video-sharing sites, podcasts, widgets, virtual worlds, and more. Billions of people around the world use social media to share information and make connections. On a personal level, social media allows you to communicate with others like friends and family, learn new things, develop your interests, and be entertained. During the world pandemic, People used social media to seek information about the COVID-19 crises. It resulted in health behaviour change and helped mitigate and manage the virus threats in the absence of a vaccine, screening, or testing kits.

Digital innovation to combat COVID-19: In the 3rd phase of the global pandemic, digital technologies have captured our imagination for their potential to support us in the fight against COVID-19. Before the current COVID- health, education, social and economic crisis, the most visible uses of emerging technologies, such as Artificial Intelligence, have been their applications in entertainment, in increasing productivity and convenience. Now, however, the potential of digital technologies to go beyond that have been revealed to the larger public. Emerging technologies such as Artificial Intelligence (AI) help to expedite the development of a vaccine; predict which public health measures would be most effective; and to keep the public updated with scientific information. They have also allowed us to move much of our lives online, maintaining economic and education systems when most people are staying home and helping us to remain connected to one another. Yet, not all regions and social groups are equally able to harness the potential of digital technologies to combat the virus. The digital and knowledge divides have always existed, but in a situation where many people have to stay home, it transforms from a disadvantage to a debilitating disability. Work is needed in the long-term to increase access to digital technologies, and in the short term, to ensure that lack of access does not translate into an inability to continue daily life.

Use of Mobile Application to Manage the COVID-19 Pandemic: During the pandemic private and government institution has made many mobile applications to combat Covid 19, that very helped full to protect coronavirus of people. On the other hand as an international organisation the COVID-19 pandemic UNESCO is supporting efforts to develop and deploy AI-enabled mobile app solutions to mitigate COVID-19 which respect fundamental rights, including data protection and privacy. A number of countries have developed and deployed mobile applications with different levels of Human Rights safeguards for users. UNESCO is supporting efforts of the Quebec Institute for Artificial Intelligence (MILA), a non to develop and deploy an open-source peer-to-peer solution, currently one of the rare solutions that protects fundamental rights related to data protection and privacy.

The application will empower individuals to monitor their own health by alerting them if they have crossed paths with an infected individual, provide them with a real-time evaluation of their exposure to COVID-19, provide behavioural messages, in consultation with UNESCO, and facilitate easy customised access to information, all while maintaining the highest standards of data and privacy protection. It will also facilitate the work of public health authorities by providing path-tracing information of voluntary, self-disclosing users, providing input into informed data-driven decisions about social distancing measures. More broadly, UNESCO advocates for the assessment of privacy, non-discrimination, and personal data protection in all ongoing initiatives which use AI to counter COVID-19.

Source: https://tinyurl.com/bdewjyu5 and https://tinyurl.com/4vf9tz66

Mobilising young innovators against COVID-19:

In the World pandemic, 6 to 30 April 2020, UNESCO, IBM, and SAP are joining forces in the organization of the global hackathon Code the Curve.

The initiative calls for young developers, innovators, data scientists, and designers to use their digital skills, creativity, and entrepreneurial spirit, and to team up to inspire digital solutions to current and future pandemic-related challenges. Through this online event, UNESCO and its partners aim to highlight how times of crisis might also engender opportunities to rethink our daily lives: imagine different forms of education and learning, step up efforts to combat the spread of disinformation, improve the quality of the information in an ethical manner, and reinforce scientific cooperation at a global scale. Participants will also have the opportunity to receive training on innovative solutions from the various organizations brought together under the umbrella of Code the Curve.

WHO Academy's mobile learning app was developed specifically for health workers and is designed to enable them to expand their life-saving skills to battle COVID-19. It delivers mobile access to a wealth of COVID-19 knowledge resources developed by WHO, including up-to-the-minute guidance, tools, training, and virtual workshops to support health workers in caring for patients infected by COVID-19 and in protecting themselves as they do their critical work. The official WHO information app. Keep the latest global health information at your fingertips. The app updates daily with the latest news, feature stories, fact sheets, disease outbreak updates, and public health emergency information. It is available in the 6 official WHO languages like Arabic, Chinese, English, French, Spanish, and Russian.

Work from Home during the COVID-19 Outbreak:

The COVID-19 outbreak has made working from home (WFH) the new way of working for millions of employees in the EU and around the world. Due to the pandemic, many workers and employers had to switch, quite suddenly, to remote work for the first time and without any preparation. Job demands refer to the physical, psychological, or socio-organizational aspects of the work whose energy-depleting process induces people to experience energy loss and fatigue, leading to stress, burnout, and health impairment. On the contrary, job resources refer to the physical, psychological, social, or organizational aspects of the job that reduce job demands while stimulating work motivation, personal growth, and development. The present job systems like work from home are fully dependent on Internet telecommunication.

The Rise of Online learning:

The COVID-19 has resulted in schools shutting all across the world. Globally, over 1.2 billion children are out of the classroom. As a result, education has changed dramatically, with the distinctive rise of e-learning, whereby teaching is undertaken remotely and on digital platforms. Research suggests that online learning has been shown to increase retention of information, and take less time, meaning the changes coronavirus have caused might be here to stay.

With this sudden shift away from the classroom in many parts of the globe, some are wondering whether the adoption of online learning will continue to persist post-pandemic, and how such a shift would impact the worldwide education market. On the other hand, before COVID-19, there was already high growth and adoption in education technology, with global investments reaching US$18.66 billion in 2019 and the overall market for online education projected to reach $350 Billion by 2025. Whether it is language apps, virtual tutoring, video conferencing tools, or online learning software, there has been a significant surge in usage since COVID-19.

Source: https://rb.gy/tjqmmj

Social media engagement of Younger:

The pandemic has not only compromised the economy and altered people's lifestyle due to lockdown and various safety measures but also deeply impacted on practice of daily lifestyle. During this time Social media has become an integral part of teens' daily life. Social media use has become even more pronounced during the pandemic because of heightened concerns and social distancing. Social media have become a ubiquitous presence in teens' daily life. Social media provide important platforms for information exchange and social interactions with minimal geographical and temporal boundaries, which contributes to social capital development and individual wellbeing. Problematic internet use in adolescents has been shown to significantly increase over the past few years, with COVID-19 pandemic lockdowns reinforcing this phenomenon globally. During the pandemic, they've oftentimes turned to social media as a positive outlet to relieve anxiety.

Digitization of the administration:

Digitization of the administration is designed to raise the convenience of the people, simplify the administration, and improve efficiency and transparency of it, through the use of IT in every field of the administration and review of existing systems and practices. During the COVID-19 crisis, many parts of administrations had to close offices and move to almost full or partial remote working. Some parts of administrations were able to carry out service as usual in all areas, including difficulties in dealing with online-based communications and forms, beneficiary contacts and some aspects of systems maintenance with the help of ICT. In addition, any part of the administration has been asked to undertake new roles providing various assistance, including financial assistance, to people on behalf of the wider government. In this way, the traditional administration has updated with digital technology. During the last two year maximum public and private administrations has continued their work online.

Digital Marketing:

Since the invention of the internet, e-commerce has grown exponentially, putting a strain on traditional brick-and-mortar stores. As we move forward and deal with the effects of COVID-19, the digital economy IS the economy. Because of the coronavirus people was more habituated to buy on the online platform and it has made a passer on e-commerce through using social media. Now with the pandemic, the internet has become a lifeline for most businesses. If there was a time for all companies to invest in digital marketing, it's now. Today from city to village maximum people are marketing on an online shops like Flipkart, Amazon etc. During the pandemic, consumers have moved dramatically toward online channels, and companies and industries have responded in turn. Many survey results confirm the rapid shift toward interacting with customers through digital channels.

Conclusion: In recent times social media is an important platform for communication and it communicates one person with many. During Covid 19 Social media was only way to have conversations, share information and create web content.From the COVID-19 crises, the administrations have changes to their previous strategy on the digitalization of administration processes. Maximum parts of administrations plan to continue work with the help of a virtual/digital environment going forward. The majority of administration indicated that they are trying to make additional changes of their IT systems for fully online to provide public benefit during COVID 19 and after the pandemic situation. All the phase of educational institution has fully run on online mode due to the corona pandemic. We all are well known that e-marketing and online jobs are increasing during the corona crisis. Lastly, I want to say the COVID 19 pandemic very badly affected in our society but the impact of this pandemic large number of people has well habituated to use social media.

References

- Chan, A. K., Nickson, C. P., Rudolph, J. W., Lee, A., & Joynt, G. M. (2020). Social media for rapid knowledge dissemination: early experience from the COVID-19 pandemic. Anaesthesia, 75(12), 1579-1582.
- Wiederhold, B. K. (2020). Social media use during social distancing. Cyberpsychology, Behavior, and Social Networking, 23(5), 275-276.
- Hussain, W. (2020). Role of social media in COVID-19 pandemic. The International Journal of Frontier Sciences, 4(2), 59-60.
- Abbas, J., Wang, D., Su, Z., & Ziapour, A. (2021). The role of social media in the advent of COVID-19 pandemic: crisis management, mental health challenges and implications. Risk management and healthcare policy, 14, 1917.
- https://en.wikipedia.org/wiki/Social_media
- https://www.tritoncommerce.com/blog/articleid/190/the-importance-of-digital-marketing-during-and-after-covid-19
- https://japan.kantei.go.jp/it/network/priorityall/6.html#:~:text=1)
- %20Digitization%20of%20the%20administration,of%20existing
- %20systems%20and%20practices.

CHAPTER THREE

An analysis of the "Make in India" program and its prospect

------*Satish Kumar Gupta**Dr.Sandeep Kumar Kesarwani*

Introduction

The manufacturing sector's high rate of growth is a significant factor in a country's rapid growth. In this context, the Indian government has launched the "Make in India" initiative in the year 2014, intending to provide a broad spectrum of support for industrial growth by enacting business-friendly regulations, enhancing the ease of doing business, and upgrading manufacturing infrastructure. This paper aims to clarify the Make in India initiative. At the same time, it discusses how the "Make in India" campaign came to be. The present scenario will be addressed in the first part, and it will be incorporated into the government's economic policy. The second part will concentrate on the state's actions. The advantages and drawbacks of the most straightforward policies will be attempted to be clarified. Finally, the implications of these policies and the final status of these steps will be disclosed in the third part.

1. Present scenario

To promote and encourage investments to develop a business partnership, the government created the Federation of Indian Chambers of Commerce and Industry (FICCI), the Digitize India Platform (DIP), and the Invest India agency. This agency creates bilateral relationships between the investor and the area in which the investments will be made, resulting in the most productive current investments. In 2020, India climbed to 67th position in the World Bank's ease of doing business index, after focusing on investors' concerns about doing business in India. The government has prepared a 98-point action plan for the provinces in this regard. The provinces and provinces of provinces were classified based on how easy it was to acquire infrastructure resources such as purchasing land for developers, purchasing electricity, receiving government permission and approval, and taxation. In addition to the fact that the government has eased restrictions on foreign direct investment in critical sectors like defence, insurance, and rail infrastructure as part of the Make in India initiative, the country has seen a significant rise in investments and investment proposals since fiscal 2015-16.

Furthermore, the government relaxed limits on foreign direct investment in critical sectors such as defence, insurance, and rail infrastructure. As a result, beginning in 2015-16, the country saw a significant rise in investments and investment proposals. In 2015, 24 of the 30 projects in the Modified Industrial Infrastructure Upgradation Scheme (MIIUS) were approved in principle, with another six projects receiving preliminary approval. In the same year, the government broadened the reach of customs tax benefits for some goods to help exporters resolve challenges with commodity shipments.

Around 2.228 new products have been added to the current list of textile products under the Merchandise Exports from India Scheme (MEIS), with up to 110 new tariffs on electronic devices. The $ 2.8 billion to $ 3.3 billion in deductibles for MEIS mainly was comprised of customs tax benefits.

Finally, the initiative to modernize and grow Intellectual Property (IP) offices aims to lower operating costs, improve accountability in the operation of the rope offices, and improve human resources at the time of submission.

2. The Prospect of Make in India

The fundamental goal of the Make in India initiative is to concentrate on job creation and skill development in 25 different sectors of the economy. It is the outcome of a few steps taken to advance in certain areas of industrial policy growth in this context.

- **Target for zero imports by 2020:** The Government wants to balance electronics imports and exports by 2020. The IT sector is expected to develop; 12.5 million people would benefit from the Government's Updated Special Incentives Scheme (MSIS) up until 2020. Several billion dollars worth of plans has been compiled and reviewed. Electronic producers are expected to follow the strategy according to the plan. The government would include 20-25 percent of the money.

- **Start-up India:** The Start-up India mission will provide entrepreneurs with bank funding and incentives. Businesses in India have announced the establishment of an "Atal Innovation Mission" (AIM) and a willingness fund to encourage new businesses. It is planned that various steps to support this initiative will be implemented. Government entrepreneurship, and to establish India as a global leader in entrepreneurship.
- **Automotive Mission Plan (AMP):** The 2016-26 Automotive Mission Plan (AMP) was announced in September 2015 by the Indian government in collaboration with the Society of Indian Automobile Manufacturers (SIAM) to become one of the country's top three automakers. The Society of Indian Manufacturers (SIAM) and the Indian Government declared a partnership in September 2015. According to the plan, India's automotive industry will be worth 260-300 billion dollars by 2026. AMP wants to make India's auto industry the "Make in India" initiative's locomotive. The German automobile industry has put much effort into this initiative. BMW, Mercedes-Benz, Audi, and other automotive behemoths are now manufacturing replacement spare parts in India. During the preliminary phase, the same companies planned to set up manufacturing in India for Asian markets. However, in the current system, the government is promoting Tata, Maruti, and Mahindra to innovate and import vehicles. In reality, it is well established that Maruti collaborated with Japan, and Mahindra began strenuous efforts in this region by acquiring Turkey's largest tractor company for tractor and agricultural production.
- **Industry Status for Jewellery:** India leads the world in jewelry sales, accounting for 29% of global sales; with a share of 6-7 percent of the economy, or 13 percent of petroleum products, the sector contributes the most to commodity exports. The jewelry sector's export amount was 19.2 billion dollars between September and April 2015. India, the world leader in diamond cutting and polishing, has advanced diamond cutting technology. Furthermore, India is one of the countries that produced the cheapest polished jewelry.
- **Impact of make in India program on Indian economy:**

Make in India and other initiatives are projected to contribute an average annual rate of 8.8% over the 2017-27 timeframe. So, "Make in India" is expected to raise the manufacturing sector's share of the economy from 16% to 25% by 2022. The program is expected to revitalize the manufacturing sector and help it become self-sustaining. Between 2011 and 2015, the sector expanded at an average annual rate of 5.77 percent. The Make in India sector is expected to expand at a pace of 12-14 percent per year. Furthermore, the Make in India entrepreneur is projected to hire approximately 100 million people by 2022.

27.497 of them have been completed by 50.442 Projects. New project plans have been considered in recent months. According to the office of the Prime Minister's initiatives, the country's dealership dropped to 7.6% in the last quarter of the fiscal year 2013-14 from a high of 8.5 percent in the last quarter of the fiscal year 2015-16. The government, which is well aware of the situation, intends to strengthen bilateral ties with Japan, Israel, and Sweden and invest heavily in attracting investment. Visions for cooperation with Turkey, Russia, and South Africa are still being developed as part of this program. Foreign direct investment inflows to the country totaled $ 40 billion in the 2015-16 fiscal year, up 29% from the previous year's $ 30.9 billion. This investment totaled 21.6 billion in the first half of the fiscal year 2016-17. This total is estimated to be 43 billion dollars as a result of the new agreements.

As a result, in fiscal 2015-16, India is ranked 16th in the World Economic Forum Competition report. The IMF lists it as the world's second-fastest-growing economy.

- **Present status in various sectors of make in India**

1. **Automotive industry** India accounts for 7% of the country's GDP. Furthermore, with a turnover of $ 145 billion in 2017, this sector is projected to be located in the country's far reaches. This government allows 100 percent foreign direct investment in the sector through automatic approval. The Indian automotive sector is expected to expand to 260-300 billion dollars by 2026, according to the 2026 automotive Mission Plan. In addition, the government has planned the National Electric Mobility Mission (NMEM) for 2020 to encourage the use of electric and hybrid vehicles in India.
2. **Aviation Market** On the 9th, India's aviation market was valued at $ 16 billion. By 2020, it will be the world's third-largest market. In the airport projects to be built, approximately 100 percent foreign direct investment

is authorized under the automatic approval program. In this regard, India has caught up with the previous year's output by 16 percent. With the introduction of low-cost air routes, the sector is expected to expand at a rapid pace. Infrastructure construction is given special attention by specializing in airports and navigation systems. Furthermore, the government takes additional measures to place India as Asia's Maintenance, Repair, and Overhaul center (MRO).

3. **IT and Electronics** India's IT industry contributes about 115-120 billion dollars to the economy, accounting for 8.1 percent of GDP. This industry employs 3.1 million employees, making it India's largest private employer. The Electronics System Design & Manufacturing (ESDM) Sector is worth between $90 and $95 billion. After the launch of the Make in India project, the government has received $1.716 billion from various companies. The Israeli and Japanese markets account for a significant portion of these deals.

The Digital India Initiative aims to digitize and deliver essential government services through the internet. In this sense, this industry aspires to take advantage of a variety of opportunities. The government intends to build semiconductor manufacturing plants in the region. Two plants in Gujarat and Uttar Pradesh are expected to open in this section. Furthermore, the government will invest $ 10 billion in the production of computer jeeps. India will also invest $400 million in the development of microprocessors. A particular Electronic Innovation Fund was established to promote venture capital funds by entrepreneurs in the region.

1. **Chemicals and Oil** The chemical industry contributed 2.1 percent to the country's GDP, with annual revenue of $ 144 billion. India is Asia's largest international chemical producer and the worlds sixth-largest.
2. **Textile Goods** India is the world's second-largest producer of textile products. The industry sector accounts for 14% of the country's manufacturing production and 4% of the country's GDP. By 2021, the industry is estimated to be worth $ 141 billion.
3. **Construction** The construction industry accounts for more than 10% of India's GDP. It employs 35 million people and manages $ 126 billion in savings. At the second stage, it is the country's second-largest foreign direct investment market. As a result, the government has once again eased some of the limits on direct foreign investment for investors. The

Turkish government has taken significant measures in this regard. The visit of Turkish President Recep Tayyip Erdogan to India is significant.

In India, there are 19 million housing units. In India's rural areas, there are projected to be 48 million units. For all Indian descent, the Indian government introduced "housing for everyone" before 2022. Significant investment opportunities arose. In Turkey, the same project began in 2004. In this sense, the TOKI project launched in Turkey is being discussed as a role model for India.

7. **Food Industry** India's food industry ranks fifth globally in each category (imports, exports, and utilities). In addition, the Public-Private Partnerships (PPP) model was developed with a $ 1.5 billion investment and a 42 mega gardens park. India's strategic geographical position and proximity to food importers make it an ideal destination for processed food exports. India is the world's largest meat processing center and the world's second-largest wheat and rice producer. As a result, the food processing industry provides appealing investment opportunities. Additionally, customers can purchase high-protein, low-fat, and organic foods.

3.Conclusion

The Make in India initiative, which was launched under the Vigyan Bhavan on December 29, 2014, in various industrial fields as a result of workshops hosted by the industrial policy and development department and attended by cabinet ministers and government heads. Wieden Kennedy was in charge of the campaign's design. During the project, 25 brochures and a web portal were published. Foreign capital regulations in different sectors were relaxed before the legislation's introduction. In addition, the world was exposed to the online platform, and India's most comprehensive initiative began.

The program began in less than four years, but its global impact was enormous. The government has frequently made every effort to provide investors with a "zero defect-zero impact" strategy, which has attracted considerable interest from foreign investors. Sweden, in reality, has been aiming to join the country market with significant investments in recent years. Through this initiative and politics, the program will lead the program in a decade of innovation and, eventually, the nation in a severe way.

After 2026, India will unavoidably join the top five economies globally, as predicted with the numbers previously. In addition to these benefits, the system has several drawbacks. As far as is known, India was a country whose economy was based on an ancient structure. TATA is an excellent example of this. It is possible to state that. Of course, Tata's long-term attempt to discourage foreign investment has harmed the country's economy. It is unlikely that a branded car will be seen on the streets for another 5-6 years. In reality, it has set a target to play a monopoly position in production in some fields, and it is in direct conflict with the government. Of course, this is only one example of the late-period aging system. Such a large number of such firms has resulted in India's long-term global market opening and severe political backwardness. In reality, the dispute with Pakistan has resulted in a fully closed strategy. This dissolution is expected to end in the coming years, and India will resume a significant position in global politics.

Second, several papers have been published in recent time that makes severe comparisons. Between Prime Minister Narendra Modi and Turkish President Recep Tayyip Erdogan, Erdogan is a hierarchical and conventional chief from the right side of the country. The government has filled in various institutions such as organizations, societies, and so on since he became Prime Minister in 2004. In general, this situation led to the observation of other people's policies directed against the nation. In reality, they are dissatisfied with these organizations, and some have begun to air their grievances in the open media. Fethullah Gulen's coup attempt, which was close to the governors of these countries, was quickly expelled from the region. In reality, Turkey is still cleaning up the scum from the failed coup attempt. There is plenty of research in the past 100 years, including in the presence of lawmakers. I am trying to say that Prime Minister of India has recently appeared to put different levels of citizens and groups in the state close to him. We should agree that Erdogan's latest decisions and ethnic and religious government policies are similar to those he has taken since taking office. Indeed, the president's recent announcement of Muslim elections in Uttar Pradesh indicates that this situation will worsen in the future. Of course, these are all hypotheticals, and there are only a few examples of this subject. Nevertheless, just as we have heard, there are more than 100 of these living examples.

Finally, if India is to play an active role in global affairs, domestic politics must be resolved adequately. Otherwise, investments would be transient due to a lack of confidence in the default domestic politics. In reality, the Make in India program covers this: invest for the first 25 years, then specialize in every way to become the world's largest producer and innovator. In reality, in the defence industry, the slogan "Make in India to Made in India" has already begun to take hold. So, if India is trying to gain power with such an extensive program on the ground, it must be unequivocal in its bilateral relations. However, as we have seen over the last two years, governments have difficulty engaging with and sharing this initiative with states where India has previously had issues. Turkey is the most basic example of this. The flags of Armenia and the Republic of South Cyrus are the most visible examples of propaganda and propaganda on every street as Erdogan arrives in Delhi. When Erdogan arrived in India, the Indian government was determined to make significant changes. The second is the most prominent example of Sino-American ties. In reality, the same issue arose during the interviews with Chinese officials. Furthermore, the news was published twice in the European press, which has a shaky relationship with Ukraine.

Nonetheless, this program continues to be the world's largest state-led initiative. We will keep an eye on this program in the coming years, and we will all be able to see, as it appears, how the nation progresses and becomes a global force.

REFERENCES

- Article[1]. Ferhat Cagri Aras 1 Process of "Make in India" Initiative Program , (Journal Of Humanities And Social Science, Volume 22, Issue 11, Ver. 12 (November. 2017) PP 22-26, e-ISSN: 2279-0837, p-ISSN: 2279-0845.)
- Article[2]. Neelofar Kamal, Make in India : A Roadmap for Sustainable Growth, International Journal of Business Administration and Management. ISSN 2278-3660 Volume 7, Number 1 (2017)

Websites

[1]. www.makeinindia.com

[2]. https://www.worldwidejournals.com/paripex/recent_issues_pdf/2016/April/make-in-india--new-paradigm-for-socioeconomic-growth-in-india_April_2016_6065510490_8010156.pdf

[3]. https://www.pppinindia.gov.in/

[4]. https://amity.edu/UserFiles/admaa/79382Paper%206.pdf [5]. http://www.indianeconomy.net/splclassroom/182/what-is-automatic-route-and-approval-route-in-fdi/

[6]. http://niti.gov.in/content/atal-innovation-mission-aim

[7]. https://www.worldbank.org/en/news/press-release/2019/10/24/doing-business-india-

top-10-improver-business-climate-ranking

[8]. https://www.pmindia.gov.in/en/major_initiatives/make-in-india/

[9]. https://pib.gov.in/PressReleasePage.aspx?PRID=1694804

[10]. http://ficci.in/about-ficci.asp

[11]. https://www.financialexpress.com/about/make-in-india/

[12]. http://www.narendramodi.in/pm-launches-make-in-india-global-initiative-6644

[13]. https://byjus.com/free-ias-prep/make-in-india/

[14]. http://www.business-standard.com/article/economy-policy/make-in-india-the-story- so-far116021200338_1.html

CHAPTER FOUR

Outcomes of COVID 19 featured by students of School Education System in Punjab Province

-------*Ms.Kinza Hafeez**Dr. Saira Taiba***Dr.Tariq Mehmood****Furqan Majeed

Introduction:

As of February 24, 2021, severe acute respiratory syndrome Coronavirus, 2 (SARS-CoV-2) has infected more than 112 million people across the world and more than 2.49 million died because of this virulent disease

Immediate lockdowns had been initiated across the whole world. Its consequences on health, welfare, business, and other parts of daily life are felt throughout society and by all people living in this global village. As there is no vaccine available for this disease, therefore reducing the rate of infection (i.e., flattening the curve) is our first priority. Prevention of getting this infection is the best way to accomplish this intention. Therefore, Quarantine is the best way to prevention of getting an infection by this deadly virus. Quarantine is the disconnection and limitation of movement of people who have might be exhibited to this disease to determine if they turn out to be ill for dropping the possibility of infecting other individuals in the population (CDC 2017). The method of Quarantine has been used as a major measure for precaution from getting such kind of contagious diseases since previous many centuries. The spread of infectious diseases such as cholera and plague have been proven to be greatly reduced by using this technique of quarantine (Brooks *et al.* 2020, Twu*et al.* 2003, Barbera*et al.* 2001). SARS-CoV-2 spreads from one individual to another individual via close contact and causes infection of COVID-19. The virus of COVID 19 might spread in the course of aerosols emitted through respiratory droplets. It has been found through some studies that SARS-CoV-2 virus'sRNA was present in air samples (Guo ZD *et al.* 2020, Chia PY *et al.* 2020 and Santarpia JL *et al.* 2020), but not found in other studies (Cheng V *et al.* 2019, Wong SCY *et al.* 2020, Faridi S *et al.* 2020 and On SWX *et al.* 2020)

However, finding RNA viruses is not necessarily indicative of replication-competent and infection-competent (viable) viruses that could be transmitted from one person to another. The exact measurement of social distance among individuals is undecided. For the present and expected future (ie, until a safe and effective vaccine or treatment, becomes available), we will have to follow COVID-19 prevention. This will continue to rely on non-pharmaceutical intercessions, including pandemic improvement in community settings (Qualls N *et al.* 2017 and Feng S *et al.* 2020).

Discussion & Presentation

Preventive measures to avoid COVID 19 include social distancing, quarantine, limitation in public places, local and international travel ban, closure of schools and lockdown ((Fauci et al., 2020). Prevalent the spread of the deadly virus and public precautionary measures have obstructed all educational activities. In addition to this, it highly affected business communities around the world, health and tourism. A huge number of schools, colleges and universities around the world have either delayed courses or started virtual learning environments. Most of them had also dropped all events like workshops, conferences, sports and other activities (Sahu, 2020). To reduce the effect of lockdown on students' life, UNESCO supported all of the countries to continue education through distance learning. This organization facilitates underprivileged countries to pursue education through digital media (Pragholapati, 2020).

Like other countries government of Pakistan had also imposed a nationwide smart lockdown as announced in March 2020. However, it has much affected different zones across the country, predominantly the students and education sector. Similarly, during this period of quarantine for prevention of getting an infection of COVID- educational activities have been frozen and have taken a major excise on the mental health of students (Cao *et al.*, 2020) causing significant depression, social tension and behavioral changes (Brooks *et al.*, 2020) as it is natural for a human being to get an elevated level of anxiety and stress as a result of any extraordinary situation (Roy D. *et al.* 2020). Research shows that these consequences can have harmful social and behavior changes in the life of students, especially those who do not have basic facilities that will further increase the likelihood of inequalities in the country's education sector (Van Lancker W *et al.* 2020). In ancient times such as during 1918 Pandemic teachers use tangible objects like speller boards and alphabets to teach their students and they also used to send assignments at their homes (Glass LM *et al.* 2008). However, there are mixed responses about the impact online education has on the student's learning ability, intellectualism, and education. Some authors believe that through e-learning students get the opportunity to improve their computer skills, on the other hand, different researchers argued that the absence of in-person interaction between student-teacher results in a decline in instructional effectiveness among students (Chen *et al.*, 2010). Although students have started E-learning by using different display places even before the pandemic in Pakistan still they were not very comfortable and used to of such VLEs (Baigent *al.*, 2019). Though this pandemic has obliged all students to use such platforms leading to more psychological sufferings among students (Anzar*et al.*, 2020).

Objectives:

Therefore, the purpose of this study is to evaluate and analyze the changes in the life pattern of students during the pandemic, their mental health after months of social distancing and self-isolation/ smart lockdown. It also focuses on the influence of public health / educational policies on students, belonging to the different backgrounds of educational fields, and the productivity of e-learning.

Methodology:

This potential inspectional study was conducted in a public school of Burewala from January 20, 2021, to 20 February 2021. There were 100 students. Among them, 20were female and 80 male students, those students were selected from grades 8th, $9^{th}$and 10th in a regional Government public school. Inclusion criteria were that all students who were quarantined at their homes for social distancing to avoid getting an infection of COVID 19 from March 14, 2020, to September 14, 2020, then from November 25, 2020, to January 18, 2021. All students were aged between 13 years to 18 years. After written permission from the school education department, a questionnaire was given to all those students. They were asked about effects on their health, mental wellbeing, the effectiveness of online classes at home and financial effects during the whole period of quarantine. They were asked to tick in the respective column of side effects. All of those effects were written in the questionnaire. After completion of all questionnaires, the data were analyzed according to the percentage of side effects among all people. Then, a graph was drawn on MS Excel 2007 to check the proportion of side effects in all people.

Results:

A sum of 100 students was quarantined for prevention of getting COVID- 19 infection from March 14, 2020, to September 14, 2020, then from November 25, 2020, to January 18, 2021. As the Government of Pakistan closed all public and private schools for the purpose of self-isolation to avoid chances of getting COVID- 19 infection, therefore those students were included in this study. The mean age of people was 15 years. The majority of students had ages between 14- 16 years. Gender distribution demonstrated male predominance. This self-isolation period impacted much on students. Among these effects, 12 (12%) students faced severe financial difficulties out of 100 students, while 18 (18%) students featured moderate financial crises, 30(30%) students had mild trouble financially and the remaining 40(40%) students did not face any financial difficulty. The living environment of 25(25%) students was severely changed, while of 20(20%) students was moderately changed, 22(22%) students had a mild change in their environment of life and 15(15%) students answered none in a column of change in their living environment. Severe behavioral variations arose in 22(22%) students while 29(29%) students got affected behaviorally up to moderate level, 32(32%) students had mild changes in their behavior and 17(17%) had no changes in their behavior. 52 (52%) students thought that online classes via zoom or other social media sources are severely ineffective, while 40(40%) individuals say online classes are moderately productive, 8(8%) students considered online classes ineffective up to mild level among 100. 90 (90%) students think workload will increase after opening of institutions, while 7(7%) students say workload will increase up to a moderate level. 3(3%) students say workload will increase up to a gentle level. Severe fear of getting COVID- 19 infection was found in 54(54%) students, 30(30%) students had moderate fear, while 12 (12%) students faced mild fear of getting infection and 4(4%) students did not fear. Moderate anxiety was found only in 1(1%) students, 8(8%) had mild anxiety and 91(91%) students did not feel any anxiety during this time Span. 5(5%) students felt depressed severely, while 12(12%) students had moderate depression, 33(33%) faced mild levels of depression, and 50(50%) students did not feel any depression during this time period. 30(30%) students had difficulty in concentration on their task, while 36(36%) students experienced the moderate difficulty of concentrating, 19(19%) students faced mild difficulty of concentrating and 15(15%) did not face any difficulty of concentrating. The sleeping pattern of 36(36%) students was disturbed up to a severe level, 36(36%) had the moderate difficulty of concentrating, 19(19%) students had the mild difficulty of concentrating and 15(15%) students did not face any difficulty of concentrating on a task. **5-Table1: Participants' answers on different aspects they faced during COVID 19 quarantine period at their homes.**

Sr. No.	Effects	Answered severe in %age (N=100)	Answered moderate in %age (N=100)	Answered mild in %age (N=100)	Answered None in %age (N=100)
1.	Financial Difficulties	12	18	30	40
2.	Changes in living environment	25	20	22	33
3.	Behavioral change	22	29	32	17
4.	Online classes are ineffective	52	40	08	00
5.	Work load will increase after quarantine period	90	07	03	00
6.	Fear of getting COVID- 19 infection	54	30	12	04
7.	Anxiety	00	01	08	91
8.	Depression	05	12	33	50
9.	Difficulty of concentrating	30	36	19	15
10.	Disruptions to sleeping pattern	36	30	22	12

Participants answers on different aspects they faced during COVID 19 quarantine period at their homes.

Discussion:

Public health protocols were implemented to reduce the number of COVID- 19 cases, but these preventive evaluations had caused several results. Usually, school students are considered more susceptible to different concerns in daily school life.In our study it was monitored that female students were more affected than male students due to this pandemic. Another study shows that emotional discomfort is more common in female individuals (Lau *et al.*, 2010). However, in another study it has been found that level of anxiety, depression and tension due toCOVID 19 is not related to a specific gender (Cao *et al.*, 2020).

Our study focuses on the effects of pandemic-related alterations on the mental health and well-being of this specific group of students. Our results put forward a significant negative impact of the COVID-19 epidemic on a variety of health, academic, financial and lifestyle-related effects. By carrying out this study with the help of a questionnaire, we found that most of the contributors were experiencing an enlarged level of depression and anxiety due to the COVID-19 pandemic. Most of the students' population developed these mental disturbances because of a lack of communication and social distancing (Xiao, 2020). In another research conducted in China, the psychological effect in students' communities was assessed and demonstrated that 25% of students suffer from anxiety (Cao *et al.*, 2020).

Among the effects of the pandemic known, the most important was worrying about one's own health and the health of loved ones, followed by trouble in concentrating on the specific subject matter and another daily life routine. These findings are aligned with recent research in China. They also found concerns relating to the health of oneself and of family members being highly prevalent among the general population during the pandemic. Difficulty in concentrating was commonly stated by our participants. It has previously been shown to adversely affect students' confidence in them (Martin JM *et al.* 2010) which has identified correlations to increased stress and mental health (Zuckerman DM 1989). This pandemic has impacted students' sleeping patterns as well correlated with another study (Denovan A *et al.* 2017). Corona around the whole world has not only affected daily life of people, but many countries and industries have to face financial crises ahead. This has reflected potential financial crises in the lives of students as well. Social distancing and limited traveling across the globe have limited the students with lower financial resources. Students may be facing financial problems which include debts, loans, housing, application fees, insufficiency of books and other study material. For a previous long period of time educational institutes had been shifted to online classes instead of physical classes (Witze,2020) These financial crises have also increased dropouts from schools.

As suggested by a recent Italian study we also have to assess the population's stress levels and psychosocial adjustment to plan for necessary support mechanisms, especially during the recovery phase, as well as for similar events in the future (De Girolamo G *et al.* 2020, Zhou J *et al.* 2020 and Shore JH *et al.* 2020).

COVID-19 & Pakistan

Corona Vaccine: There is good news for Pakistanis that action on vaccine vaccination in the country has started. And for this purpose, China has endowed as a gift of 5 Lac doses. The regulatory body of Pakistan has approved three types of vaccines for the country. It is mentionable that training to medical staff has given regarding vaccine of China, "Sino farm". Like the rest of the world, here front-line workers of medical staff are being vaccinated, especially to those who are working or serving in Corona Wards. It is an official report that many millions of doses will start to reach next month (in March). Furthermore, it is being stated that Govt. will provide vaccines free to the public. Anyhow, private companies are also allowed to import this vaccine which is good news but it will be challenging for Govt. & for ruling authorities to control the prices of vaccines. (MunawarMirza, 14th February 2021). Now Govt. of Pakistan has announced that after Para-medical staff, vaccines for old citizens will be provided preferably to the 65 years old citizens freely. Now they can register by sitting in their homes just dialing or sending s.m.s to 1166 service. After this, they will be vaccinated of covid-19, free of cost, near their home center.

Rumors about covid-19 Vaccine

It is a great tragedy with our country that whenever any technology or vaccine is being used or introduced for the welfare of the general public. Rumors are spread about its use. When wheat from the United States of America was imported, at that time such rumors were spread, similarly when use of iodine salt was proposed to decrease the rate of thyroid diseases, then such rumors were also spread due to this fertility rate of production is being decreased. Now at that time, in the whole world, only two countries have poliovirus, are Afghanistan and Pakistan. The main reason of that poliovirus was also rumors. In actuality, the rumors of poliovirus have no reality. And these vaccines do not decrease the fertility rate in children who are being vaccinated.

It is merely a rumor that R N A vaccines change D.N.A. In actuality, the RNA vaccine does not affect our DNA system. But through RNA, immunity is trained so that in the situation of attack defensive system could defend in power. In different countries, different pharmaceutical companies are preparing vaccines that are useful in all aspects. As concerned the vaccine which is more useful in all aspects, actually, that vaccine is available so the available vaccine will be considered as useful because the basic function of all vaccines is to train the defensive system for immunity. There are different doubts regarding the vaccine of China, it should be noted that the technology of the China vaccine is used; this is the oldest and certified technology i.e. to introduce the dead virus for the defensive system. (Rizvi Dr. Nadeem Prof. 28th March 2021)

Aasterzanika Vaccine

Aasterzanika Vaccine is approved by the Government of Pakistan, due to this vaccine; few cases are reported of blood clots after being vaccinated. But this vaccine is applied on millions of people. If few cases are reported, these cases may be accidental. Therefore about the Aasterzanika vaccine, no final opinion can be set about its usefulness or loss. World Health Organization also recommended to different countries after a few cases of blood clots that its use might not be stopped. About covid-19treatment, the advancement is that with the help of vaccines, this epidemic disease may be controlled. Still, there is no medicine prepared through which covid-19 patients might be treated well without vaccination.(Rizvi Dr. Nadeem Prof. 28th March 2021)As concerning the use of vaccination, if fourteen days have passed after the covid-19 virus attack, then vaccination may be done. Some people say that our immunity power is strong and we have anti-bodies in our body to defend our system. The why vaccine is vaccinated? It should be remembered that when any army is prepared against the enemy for a fight, Its divisions are formed in different groups and shapes, e.g. armed division, infantry division etc. Similarly Allah Almighty has formed different groups and different levels in human immunity. Similarly, there is cellular immunity have memory T cells that recognize enemy viruses. As virus inters in body, these notify to body for action. (Rizvi Dr. Nadeem Prof. 28th March 2021)

Vaccination in Children

As concerning vaccination in children, there are very few chances to be affected by the covid-19 virus in children, therefore vaccination is being done from 18 years to 80 years old persons only. And we have data of that age group of also. The benefits of vaccination are how much, about these benefits; still it may not be assured about this context. And in the present condition, the children will not be vaccinated. As concerned the death rate in children, although the death rate in children is very low but the death of one child is also a not common matter. Therefore, S.O.Ps must be followed to avoid from covid-19. The fact is that in children, in schools & colleges, S.O.Ps are being followed strictly than elders. |If in the country, people are vaccinated from 70 to 80 percent then in the majority of people, immunity power will be created against covid-19. (Rizvi Dr. Nadeem Prof. 28th March 2021)

To control virus effects with the vaccine, all scientific steps that are being done, surely these are important. But these strategies may be helpful for human being but now, it will be seen that after vaccination and taking precautions, can we become successful to satisfy human psychology and its spirit. It is the need of society that we should keep people physically healthful and these should be powerful and strong in a psychological and spiritual manner. If we can control this calamity with science, technology, medical development or material resources then we can control this virus up till now. It is need of time that specialists of neuropsychologists should give their expert opinion openly so that human being could save their bodies with their spirits to eschew humanity from this dangerous calamity according to their own creed and religions. In this context, it is very important thing that we should spread spiritual teachings rather than depending on scientific and recent material philosophy so that man could become powerful psychologically and spiritually with controlling physical diseases. Due to this calamity, in the majority of the population, negative emotions can be seen apparently. And emotions of sympathy with others are also becoming effective. Due to this long-term disease, fear and tension is spreading to ineffective families. Feeling of uncertainty situations of spreading pandemic disease has created such symptoms of uncertainty in children, young and aged persons, due to this, tension, fear, boredom and sadness can be seen. Due to this pandemic disease, millions of people have been affected. These people are either sick or becoming die with the passage of time. (Rao Sarwar Muneer, 4th April 2021)

Coronavirus is such virus that is affecting human beings of the world on large scale. It is suggested by health authorities to adopt health precautions e.g. washing hands, social distance and wearing masks but still, the disease could not be controlled. The process of vaccination is also continued since many months ago but due to this action, the disease could not be controlled. It seems that human beings of the world will have to face for next many years.

Effects of Corona Virus on Business

Corona has affected our daily lives, business, trade and transportation & communication resources at large scale. In many countries, there is a problem to continue the production process of industries. From these products, food, medicine, tourism, electronics & so many other industries of things are involved. Economically preparation of necessary things is also in low speed. And due to less cash flow, the trade cycle is also affected seriously. Shortage of social meetings, closure of visiting places, parks, gymnasium, swimming pools & other visiting places are increasing social problems. Ban and another strict lockdown on air travel also affected the aviation industry that has been also affected the refreshment psychology of common people. In many countries of the world development work has stopped. All governments have concentrated & resources to save the cities from this pandemic situation. The third wave of the corona is more dangerous so we should be careful and adopt all precautions steps. In Saudi Arabia, there is a lockdown situation, while Tanzania, Brazil, Spain has declared an emergency situation. Britain has declared lockdown for one month. In French lockdown for two weeks, in Germany curfew for 4 weeks, Italy& whole Europe totally closed. In Australia & Canada also totally lockdown policy is adopted. In the whole world, nearly one year has been spent in this situation. Now on airports of Dubai, Abu Dhabi, America & Europe shows that these are the graveyard of airplanes because they are covered with dust and clay. Now the administration is saving expenses of its cleanliness.

According to scholars' research & our religious beliefs tell us that is a single prayer offered in Ka'aba reward will be given one lakh prayers and one prayer in mosque Nabavi, there will be fifty thousand prayers reward will be given. And if Muslims perform Hajj with Umrah collectively, then his sins are removed from a person's account or balance. This bonus is also closed for more than 80 percent of people. Now we cannot celebrate our small happiness openly. As the marriage clubs and celebrations are banned.

In houses, social distance is also being kept. Now going to the invitation and calling for an invitation becomes difficult. Visit and outing programs have become a dream. Anyhow, in person's views, with worldly use of medicine, there should repentance of our wills from Almighty Allah, without this, humanity cannot save from this pandemic calamity. This pandemic situation has also opened the real situation of scientific and medical development because capital, properties and status are remained unsuccessful to cure the virus or germs. (Rao Sarwar Muneer, 4th April 2021)

Hypocrisy of Pakistani Govt. regarding Policies of covid-19

In Pakistan, Due to the third wave of covid-19, the Government of Pakistan has closed educational institutions from 14th March 2020 in big seven cities of Punjab and then two more cities Sargodha and Sheik purawere added for shutting down. But other cities of Punjab have opened their educational institutions in a covid-19 wave. The hypocrisy of Punjab Govt. may be imagined from this order that shops and other business centers are declared in official order to remain close two days in Saturday and Sunday for all cities except medical stores, puncture shops and hotels of public places. This closure is ordered to all cities of Punjab large & small cities. Here the difference is that smart lockdown is implanted to close but educational institutions are not the same enclosure of big and small cities because in big cities educational institutions are closed while in small cities educational institutions are working without considering the third wave of covid-19.

This shows that there is a difference in the preference of the lives of people of large cities and the lives of people of small cities in the eyes of ruling authorities. This is a reality because all government officials of different departments of the same scale are not getting the same salaries and allowances in all cities of Pakistan. This clearly denotes that policies of government are not the same regarding allowances and basic pay scales.

Conclusion:

In nutshell, it may be stated that most villagers are safe from Coronavirus, not because of adopting safety measures but actually the matter is quite different from the scene. Actually, they remain from distances and work in their own fields; this keeps them away from others even during their daily routine. It has been observed that in cities, many people are affected by COVID-19 because of rush and mixing in markets due to limited shopping hours. Anyhow, it may be stated that during the pandemic situation of covid-19, the majority remains safe due to limited shopping periods and strict lockdown policies. Therefore, in Pakistan, the death cases remained very few as compared to the death cases of other countries. In fact, it was the blessing of God otherwise, in Pakistan, the facilities were not in excess like developed ones. Anyhow, for more safety, we need to step up our support to the school system, protect education as an essential service, and preserve the budget for education. COVID-19 affects everyone, but we cannot let the youngest and most vulnerable members of society suffer from a crisis that threatens their present and their future. We have to strengthen curricula and support teachers to facilitate rapid catch-up with learning losses. We also need to assess the level of stress, depression, anxiety, and behavioral change. After successful assessment, we need to develop coping strategies for wellbeing and training of students and teachers as well.

References:

- World-O-Meter (2021), COVID-19, coronavirus pandemic 2020, https://www,worldometers.info/coronavirus/ (accessed February 24, 2021).
- CDC (2017), Quarantine and Isolation. USA. Retrieved from https://www.cdc.gov/quarantine/index.html.
- Brooks, (2020). The psychological impact of quarantine and how to reduce it: rapid review of the evidence. Lancet.https://doi.org/10.1016/S0140-6736 (20)30460-8.
- Twu, S.J., Chen, T.J., Chen, C.J., Olsen, S.J., Lee, L.T., Fisk, T., Hsu, K.H., Chang, S.C., Chen, K.T., Chiang, I.H., Wu, Y.C., Wu, J.S., Dowell, S.F., (2003). Control measures for severe acute respiratory syndrome (SARS) in Taiwan, Emerging infectious diseases 9(6), 718–720.https://doi.org/10.3201/eid0906.030283.
- Barbera, J., Macintyre, A., Gostin, L., Inglesby, T., et al., (2001). Large-scale quarantine following biological terrorism in the United States: scientific examination, logistic and legal limits, and possible consequences. JAMA 286 (21), 2711–2717. https://doi.org/10.1001/jama.286.21.2711.
- Roy, D., Tripathy, S., (2020) Study of knowledge, attitude, anxiety & perceived mental healthcare need in Indian population during COVID-19 pandemic. Asian J.,Psychiatry.https://doi.org/10.1016/j.ajp.2020.102083.

- Guo ZD, Wang ZY, Zhang SF, et al. Aerosol and surface distribution of severe acute respiratory syndrome coronavirus 2 in hospital wards, Wuhan, China, 2020. Emerg Infect Dis 2020; published online April 10, DOI:103201/eid2607200885.
- Chia PY, Coleman KK, Tan YK, et al. (2020) Detection of air and surface contamination by severe acute respiratory syndrome coronavirus 2 (SARS-CoV-2) in hospital rooms of infected patients medRxiv2020; published online April 9, DOI:10.1101/2020.03.29.20046557.
- Santarpia JL, Rivera DN, Herrera V, et al. (2020) Transmission potential of SARS-CoV-2 in viral shedding observed at the University of Nebraska Medical Center. medRxiv2020; published online March 26, DOI:10.1101/2020.03.23.20039446 (preprint).
- Cheng V, Wong S-C, Chen J, et al. (2020)Escalating infection control response to the rapidly evolving epidemiology of the coronavirus disease 2019 (COVID-19) due to SARS-CoV-2 in Hong Kong. Infect Control HospEpidermal; 41: 493–98.
- Wong SCY, Kong RT-S, Wu TC, et al. (2020)Risk of nosocomial transmission of coronavirus disease 2019: an experience in a general ward setting in Hong Kong. J Hosp Infect 2020; 105:119–27.
- Faridi S, Niazi S, Sadeghi K, et al.(2020) A field indoor air measurement of SARS-CoV-2 in the patient rooms of the largest hospital in Iran. Sci Total Environ2020; 725:138401.
- Ong SWX, Tan YK, China PY, et al. (2020)Air, surface environmental and personal protective equipment contamination by severe acute respiratory syndrome coronavirus 2 (SARS-CoV-2) from a symptomatic patient. JAMA; 323:1610–12.
- 9. Qualls N, Levitt A, Kanade N, et al.(2017) Community mitigation guidelines to prevent pandemic influenza: United States. MMWR Recomm; 66:1–34.
- 10. Feng S, Shen C, Xia N, Song W, Fan M, (2020) Cowling BJ. Rational use of face masks in the COVID-19 pandemic. Lancet Respir Med; 8:434–36
- 11. Fauci AS, Lane HC, Redfield RR (2020).Covid-19—navigating the uncharted.
- 12. Sahu P (2020). Closure of universities due to Coronavirus Disease 2019 (COVID-19): impact on education and mental health of students and academic staff. Cureus, 12 (4)
- 13. Pragholapati A (2020). COVID-19 IMPACT ON STUDENTS.

- 14. Cao W, Fang Z, Hou G, Han M, Xu X, Dong J, Zheng J (2020).The psychological impact of the COVID-19 epidemic on college students in China. Psychiatry research, 112934
- 15. Brooks SK, Webster RK, Smith LE, Woodland L, Wessely S, Greenberg N, Rubin GJ (2020). The psychological impact of quarantine and how to reduce it: rapid review of the evidence, The Lancet.
- 16. Van Lancker W, Parolin Z (2020). COVID-19, school closures and child poverty: a social crisis in the making, The Lancet Public Health, 5(5), e243-e244.
- 17. Glass LM, Glass RJ (2008). Social contact networks for the spread of pandemic influenza in children and teenagers, BMC public health, 8(1), 61.
- 18. Chen PSD, Lambert AD, Guidry KR (2010).Engaging online learners: The impact of Web-based learning technology on college student engagement. Computers & Education, 54(4), 1222-1232.
- 19. Baig QA, Zaidi SJA and Alam BF (2019), Perceptions of dental faculty and students of E-learning and its application in a public sector Dental College in Karachi, Pakistan, JPMA.
- 20. Anzar W, Baig QA, Afaq A, Taheer TB, Amar S (2020), Impact of infodemise on Generalized Anxiety disorder, sleep quality and depressive symptoms among Pakistani Social media users during epidemics of COVID-19. https://zenodo. org/ api/ files/ a417bc52-7e40-46fb 8a04-46ea71ce2c98/Anzar% 20et% 20al,pdf.
- 21. Lau JT, Griffiths S, Choi KC, Tsui HY (2010). Avoidance behaviors and negative psychological responses in the generalpopulation in the initial stage of the H1N1 pandemic in Hong Kong, BMC, Infectious Diseases, 10(1), 139.
- 22. Cao W, Fang Z, Hou G, Han M, Xu X, Dong J, Zheng J (2020).The psychological impact of the COVID-19 epidemic on college students in China, Psychiatry research, 112934.
- 23. Xiao C (2020). A novel approach of consultation on 2019 novel coronavirus (COVID-19)-related psychological and mental problems: structured letter therapy, Psychiatry investigation,17(2), 175.
- 24. Martin JM. (2010), Stigma and student mental health in higher education, Higher Education Res Dev. 2010 Jun; 29(3): 259–274. doi: 10.1080/07294360903470969.
- 25. Zuckerman DM. (1989) Stress, self-esteem, and mental health: how does gender make a difference? Sex Roles; 20(7-8):429–444. doi:

10.1007/BF00288001.

- 26. Denovan A, Dagnall N, Dhingra K, Grogan S. (2017) Evaluating the perceived stress scale among UK university students: implications for stress measurement and management. Stud Higher Education; 44 (1): 120–133. doi: 10.1080/03075079.2017.1340445.
- 27. Witze A (2020). Universities will never be the same after the corona virus crisis. Nature
- 28. De Girolamo G, Cerveri G, Clerici M, Monzani E, Spinogatti F, Starace F, Tura G, Vita A. (2019) Mental health in the coronavirus disease, emergency-the Italian response. JAMA Psychiatry, 2020 Apr 30;:A. doi: 10.1001/jamapsychiatry.2020.1276.
- 29. Zhou J, Liu L, Xue P, Yang X, Tang X. (2020) Mental health response to the COVID-19 outbreak in China. Am J Psychiatry; 177(7):574–575. doi: 10.1176/appi.ajp.2020.20030304.
- 30. Shore JH, Waugh M, Calderone J, Donahue A, Rodriguez J, Peters D, Thomas M, and Giese A. (2020) Evaluation of tale-psychiatry-enabled perinatal integrated care. PsychiatrServ; 71 (5):427–432. doi: 10.1176/appi.ps.201900143.
- 31-MunawarMirza (14thFebruary,2021) “On Deniel Perl Case: Strict Action of new American Administration, Sunday Magazine of Jang newspaper, p-2.
- 32-Rizvi Dr. Nadeem Prof. (28th March2021) “Sino farm kitayyari”, Multan: Jang Sunday Magazine, p-8.
- 33-Rao SarwarMuneer, (4th April,2021) “Corona Vaccine, kiawabakaelaaj hey?”, Multan: Daily Express newspaper, p-10.

CHAPTER FIVE

Online Teacher Education Programme For Higher Education School System To Present Situation Of Covid-19 Pandemic Period

------*Rajarshi Roy Chowdhury Murshidabad**Mallika Mondal*

Introduction: E-learning/online education according to Harrison 1989 is a new domain of learning that combines distance education within the practice of face-to-face instruction utilizing computer-mediated communication. Ascough (2002) suggested that online education has the following features) it provides a learning experience different than in the traditional classroom because learners are different. (b) communication is vital for computers and the Worldwide Web (c) participation in the classroom by learners are different. (d) the social dynamics of the learning environment is changed and€ discriminations and prejudice is minimized. The term e-learning has only been in existence since 1999 when the world was first utilized at a CVT system seminar other words also begin to spring up in search of an accurate description such as online learning and virtual learning however the principals behind eLearning have been will document take 2 out history and there is even evidence which suggests that early forms of e-Learning existed as far back as the 19th century. Long before the internet was launched distance courses were being offered to provide students with education on particular subjects or skills. In 1840 Isaac Pitman thought his people's shorthand via correspondence. In 1924 the first testing machine was invented. This device allowed students to taste themselves. Then in 1954 BF Skinner, a Herbert professor invented the teaching machine which enables schools to administrated programmed instruction to their students. He was not until 1960 however that the first computer boat training programme was introduced to the world.

New technologies, the internet screaming video, Netmeeting, etc. Now makes higher education more accessible and affordable for many students and for those who would have been unable to pursue higher education in a traditional in-class setting(Bianno&care-chellman,2002) consequently, online e-learning has now become an integral part of Higher Education institutions expanding curriculum . With the introduction of the computer and internet in the late 20th-century e-learning tools and delivery methods expanded the first Mac in 1980 enabled individuals to have computers in their homes, making it easier for them to learn about a particular subject and develop certain skills sets in the 2008 businesses began using e-learning to train their employees. New and experienced workers light now had the opportunity to improve upon their industry knowledge base and explain their skill sets. At home, individuals were granted access to programs that offer them the ability to learn online degrees and enrich their lives the expanded knowledge. Today e-learning is more popular than ever with counters individuals relishing the benefits that online learning can offer.

Objectives Of Study:

- Identify the relationship between e-learning and teacher education programs among Higher secondary school students.
- Identify the relation in time spent on the electronic gadgets on the online program.
- Impact the e-Learning of the covid-19 pandemic situation.
- Identify the relationship between ruler and urban areas secondary students use online mobile computers.

Literature Review :

1. Taurus, David, and Alex, (2015) investigate the challenges hindering the implementation of E-learning in Kenyan public universities. It also emerged that the implementation of E-learning in Kenya faces some challenges. These include but are not limited to inconvenient ICT and E-learning.

2. Donnelly, & McAvinia, (2012) argue that there are "many academics have had no training and little experience in the use of communications and information technology as an educational tool" p 19. Furthermore, administrative factors could contribute to minimizing the benefit of using E-learning.
3. Feeney (2001), E-learning has been the focus of recent scholarly attention. As the integration of technology into higher education becomes an institutional imperative university worldwide, the adoption of digital courses in a new E-learning Environment becomes both an organizational goal and a source of data upon which To evaluate performance. Furthermore, he states that higher education institutions face persistent challenges in the use of technology, with E-learning being the latest Technological challenge Feeney (2001).
4. Kim (2008) indicates that the challenges of technology impede the use of E-learning In higher education is faculty resistance. In contrast, other studies show factors such As technology, interaction, instructor, and quality of students were key factors to Successful E-learning (Selim, 2007, Baylor & Ritches, 2002., Volery & Lord 2000).
5. Khan, Hasan., and Clement, (2012) also found out that if teachers want to use technology in their classes successfully, they need to possess a positive attitude Towards the use of technology. For the benefits of E-learning, Clarke (2004) asserts That learners have freedom of choice over "place, pace and time" (p.32).
6. Wanjala., Khaemba, and Mukwa, (2011) advise institutions to adopt ICT Exploitation in education because these technologies are recognized worldwide as tools That facilitate.
7. Berhanu (2010) points out that promoting E-learning provides a potential and Comparative ladder for developing countries to leapfrog to the knowledge economy. It shows facilitating learning to large groups through the use of information and communication technology.
8. Bandana (2011) shows the factors related to mainly experience, positive attitudes, Confidence, enjoyment, usefulness, intention to use, motivation, and whether Students had ICT skills are all correlated.
9. Fageeh (2011) demonstrates that informants identified the facilitators and inhibitors Of E-learning previously recognized in prior research. He also shows that students Are ready to accept technology implementation and shift to an E-learning model of Education. In the same context,

10. Al-Dosari (2011) examines the faculty members' and students' perceptions of E-Learning in the English department. He observes their responses were positive and Indicated that learning improved in an E-learning environment compared to a traditional method.

Characteristics Of E-Learning:

1. Online learning: It is carried out through the internet or web-based technology, with no face-to-face interaction.

2. Empowered by digital technology: E-learning is pedagogy, empowered by digital technology.

3. Computer enhanced learning

4. Technology-enhanced learning: E-learning includes all types of technology-enhanced learning (TEL), where technology is used to support the learning process.

5. **More than online learning:** E-learning is broader in its meaning than that conveyed through the term like —online learning‖ or —online education‖ where there is no follow-up program or no interaction between the teacher and students.

6. **More than Computer-Based learning and computer-assisted instruction**: E-learning conveys broader meaning than the term CBL and CAI

7. Not synonymous with audiovisual and multimedia learning: Learning should not be described as synonymous with audiovisual learning, multimedia learning, or distance education. Although the audiovisual and multimedia Technology and distance education programs are based on the internet and a web service provided through computers, these are not identical but complementary. It means that they are supporting and interdependent or interrelated to each other.

8. **Exclusion of non-internet and non-Web Technology**: All types of non-internet and non-Web Technology are not included in learning. The entire Computer-Based instruction computer-managed instruction which are not delivered through the use of the internet, but are used for learning cannot be included in e-learning. when these techniques delivered through the internet for instruction become e-learning.

9. Confined to web-based and internet-based learning: The term e-learning should be related to that type of learning which is carried out or facilitated through web-enhanced instruction and internet-based communication like email, audio-video conferencing, and live chat.

Application of ICT: The role of the technology during covid-19 we know that technology is an essential part of our lives today's but during this pandemic technology help a man lot ichnology play a vital role such as educating people about the entire situation and remained in them to take the necessary precautions. ICT in education is the mode of education that use information and communication technology to support in hands and optimize the delivery of information. To promote improve the digital culture in schools and colleges the government has instituted the National award for the innovative use of ICT to motive teachers and educators for the innovative use of ICT in teaching-learning.

Various devices /technology in ICT includes-

1. Access of course material do remote device
2. Online digital race potteries for lectures course material and digital library.
3. Online /cloud-based academic management system
4. Learning management system.
5. Making use of a handheld computer, tablet, project the device, etc.

Different Approaches to E-Learning:

There are fundamentally two approaches to e-learning: Synchronous training and Asynchronous mode.

Synchronous Method:

Synchronous, means "at the same time," involves the interaction of participants with an instructor via the Web in real-time. Asynchronous, which means "not at the same time," allows the participant to complete the WBT at his own pace, without live interaction with the instructor.

- **Virtual Classroom:** Virtual classroom duplicates the features of a real classroom online. Participants interact with each other and instructors online, instant messaging, chat, audio and video conferencing, etc.
- **Blended Method:** Most companies prefer to use a mix of both synchronous and asynchronous e-learning methods according to their requirement. It is an amalgamation of synchronous and asynchronous learning methods.

Asynchronous Methods

- **Embedded Learning:** Embedded learning is information that is accessible on a self-help basis, 24/7. It can be delivered to the place of work, or to mobile learners. An electronic performance support system (EPSS) is a type of embedded learning. The advantage is that embedded learning offers learners the information they need whenever they need it.

Blended learning:

In this blended learning model, a combination of traditional and ICT enhanced e-learning practices are used. The teaching-learning process are so planned and executed as to present a happy combination of both the traditional classroom teaching practices and e-learning based instructions. According to the need of students and for the realization of predetermined objectives, teachers can provide knowledge of a particular subject through the use of lecture cum demonstration method and as per the need of students use ICT enhanced e-learning practices also. Thus, one can receive the benefits of both the practices of traditional and e-learning. It is predicted that blended learning will enhance the student learning experience, at the same time it also expects that the teachers should be trained as an online facilitator.

Complete e-learning:

In this complete e-learning mode, the traditional classroom teaching-learning process is totally replaced by the online or virtual classroom teaching-learning process. In this mode, there is no existence of classrooms, schools, and teaching-learning environment as happens in the traditional setup of school education. The learners are free to join the learning tasks independently with the help of properly designed e-learning courses or module-based courses through which students can learn according to their own pace. Most of the learning activities are executed entirely online, but at the same time, they may have also provided recorded information and learning packages which is available in the form of CD-ROM, DVD, etc. Therefore, e-learning activities may have two distinctive communication styles, which is as follows:

Asynchronous communication style:

In this communication style, teacher and student do not interact with each other at the same time. Students can learn when they feel comfortable doing so. The information regarding different courses or learning experiences are provided to the learners through e-mail, discussion forum, Web pages, Weblogs, wikis or through the recorded CD-ROM and DVD, or through the module-based teaching-learning process. It means that the teachers and learners do not interact simultaneously. And also students can learn according to their own pace.

Synchronous communication style:

Here the communication between the teacher and students directly takes place in an online chat room or through live audio-video conferencing.

In the present context in the covid-19 pandemic period, the educational institutions, Universities, Schools, colleges, private tuitions all are taking help of this audio-video conferencing or live chat to provide learning experiences and knowledge of their subjects to this student. Because during the lockdown period, physical presence in school or university is not possible to avoid infection of Coronavirus, so the whole world is taking help from this synchronous and asynchronous style of teaching and learning process. Only because of the Internet and Computer technology, education and many more activities are possible in this period and e-learning is one of them.

Some Initiatives at The National Level:

University Grants Commission (UGC) India's leading regulatory body for higher education, with the collaboration of the Ministry of Human Resources Development (MHRD) Under the Govt. of India, has made continuous efforts to implement e-learning initiatives even during the COVID-19 pandemic in India. Some of the essential steps to

incorporate e-learning is:

1. "Vidya-Daan," a programme focused on the crowdsourcing of teachers' content, was planned to synergies the country's innovations by supplying teachers and students from the various Metro cities to the remote areas or smallest villages for efficient quality content for e-learning that can be downloadable at anywhere, at no price and at any time.

2. Weekly Practice Program is CCT (Creative and Critical Thinking) to improve learner cognitive skills and create interest by relating learning to real-life circumstances. Teachers can also use these things to facilitate conversations and involve learners in self-learning adventures.

3. Government of India's i-Got-programme uses DIKSHA for COVID-19 training of physicians, nurses, ASHA staff, NCC, NSS, NYKS volunteers. Between April and June 2020, more than 17 lakh individual training sessions have been performed

4. PM e-Vidya declared under the Atma-Nirbhar Bharat policy that DIKSHA is the 'one nation; one digital platform' for education in India. DIKSHA is being converted into a forum for rich and diverse curriculum, linked to the e-content requirements of teachers and learners for all states and UTs, accessible via digital devices, to ensure continuity of access and learning experience.

5. Online MOOC courses related to NIOS (classes 9 to 12 of open school) are uploaded to the SWAYAM portal; about 92 courses have begun and 1.5

crore learners are enrolled. Teachers and students can access all courses modules-text, videos, evaluation questions, etc. through SWAYAM. Various online software like Zoom, Google Meet, YouTube, etc. are used for online courses and teaching.

6. We can access e-Textbooks using the e-PG Pathshala digital platform and phone app (Android, iOS, Windows) for learners, mentors, teachers, and parents. Around 600 eBooks, which includes approx. 377 digital textbooks from class I to XII and 3,500 NCERT video and audio contents, is available in different languages (Hindi English, Sanskrit, and Urdu) in the public domain.

7. Apart from the preventative measures to be taken by academic institutions to deal with the rising situation of COVID-19, UGC has undertaken all steps to ensure that all higher educational institutions maintain regular interaction with students and teachers by electronic communication and keep them completely updated so that there is no distress among students, teachers, and teachers.

Pros And Cons of E-Learning:

Advantages of E-Learning: There are a number of advantages of e-learning. First, we are using state of-the-art technology and instructional strategies. Cultures can be shared through e-learning. Disabilities can be accommodated, with or without the knowledge of other participants. Gender may not be an issue, because in many situations, gender is unknown—or it can be. Because of global access, the classroom may be the world. Nothing can replace traditional classroom teaching, but e-learning complements the process and can help reach out to the masses. The biggest advantage of e-learning lies in its ability to cover distances. For an organization that is spread across multiple locations, traditional training becomes a constraint. All trainees need to come to a classroom to get trained. Additionally, the trainees learning pace is not addressed as all trainees are treated as having equal abilities and there is little flexibility in terms of timing and completion of the course. The major advantage is the consistency that e-learning provides. e-learning is self-paced, and learning is done at the learner's pace. The content can be repeated until it is understood by the trainee. It can be made compelling and interesting with multimedia, and the trainee can be given multiple learning paths depending on his or her needs.

Disadvantages of E-Learning:

Just as glass may be half full, it may also be half empty. Which means it is not free from disadvantages to e-learning. Class members with disabilities may be functioning at a disadvantage for a number of reasons. Some participants may be technologically challenged and are hesitant to participate in full. Online discussions may inhibit class members, or they may encourage banter. One of the common disadvantages to e-learning is that some students, especially those for whom English is not their native language, have difficulty communicating and being understood. Another group of students may experience computer or technology anxiety, which may in turn impact. their learning and their final grades.

Issues and Challenges of E-Learning:

The education sector has suffered a great deal from the outbreak of COVID-19. Adopting e-learning technology without careful planning will cost a lot of money, e-learning products that are not desirable and lead to problems. It has had many negative impacts on education, some of which are as follows:

1. **Students**: Students from rural areas are neither having android and smartphones, very few Computers/Laptops due to various financial problems or constraints (MHRD, 2020). Students with disabilities are lacking behind in online classes. Learners belonging to science and medical streams are not able to practice in labs and perform experiments as they do in offline classes. They are facing various health-related issues and feel stressed as students study for long hours on smartphones/computers for online classes. Due to inconsistency an irregular schedule is harming the physical well-being of students and going for long hours of sleep.

2. **Educational Institutions:** From an infrastructural point of view, researchers have revealed that all the higher education institutions, schools, and colleges, are not ready or willing to perform online technology-based education and evaluation. All teachers from higher educational institutions are not trained or certified to teach online methods and software. Some educators are not ready for the immediate adaptation of the internet form of teaching-learning. The online teaching of a non-qualified teacher cannot reach expectations and learning goals for students.

3. **Parents**: Due to lockdown people working in the informal sector lost their job and no source of income leads to non-payment of fees. There are also other issues for parents in addition to payments for programs that the schools and universities are not prepared to offer. Who's going to pay for the data? Is there enough space and peace at home for students to focus on?

How do you teach children at home to follow digital self-restraint? There are huge obstacles for working parents and disadvantaged people in slum areas and rural areas.

4. **Miscellaneous**: The connection of electricity is again an important challenge for both teachers and students of the rural area. Inadequate Internet Penetration according to the report of TRIAL in India the internet penetration is 68.6 crores (49%), active users of the internet, in January 2020 with 138.00 crores Population in 2020 which is far less as compared to developed countries. 64.85% of Urban Area internet penetration with 48.30 crores population in urban area. 20.26 % from rural area internet penetration with 89.70 crores population in the rural area. Slow internet speed as a result students and teachers

cannot attend all the classes online and there is a lack of Social Cohesion.

5. **Difficult to motivate students**: A motivated person always gives the best on their performance. They stay always loyal and committed to their task or responsibilities. Without motivation, it becomes difficult for the students to cope up with academics as they lost their interest and they are unable to perform better in the exam.

6. **Challenges to keep track of students' progress**: In an online learning environment, it is important to help students to engage with course material which provides them ample opportunities of learning. Especially when students are learning remotely; the teacher must recognize the importance and problems of the students. Progress of students can be tracked through student attendance, periodic exam, and mock interview.

7. **Problem of electricity / Internet connectivity:** Without strong access of electricity and internet connectivity online classes cannot think. In rural areas, electricity is cut down most of the time, and there is no fixed time to availability. High internet connectivity, Wi-Fi and broadband connections that facilitate high-speed internet is not installed as it is not required daily basis by the people in rural. area, while some people can't afford it due to its high cost. Therefore, problems of electricity/internet connectivity are one of the most important challenges faced by teachers in online learning.

8. **Lack of technical /Software knowledge:** Teachers and students should be able to handle computers and software easily during online classes. Without proper knowledge of the software, they can't able to access online learning or record visual and audio. The software also required some specific requirements i.e. – space of operating hard disk, updated windows, latest graphic on a computer and many more. Without the proper

knowledge, it is quite harassing to take online classes for both teacher and student.

9. **Required more time in preparing course content:** Teaching online courses are not the same as classroom teaching. The teachers want to prepare for the course content in online teaching much more than preparing for classroom teaching.

10. **Lack of motivation in online learners:**

Motivation influences interest and changes student behavior. Online learning requires more self-attention than in classroom education. It is important for learners to be active and interested during online classes to understand the syllabus or course content.

11. **Difficult to teach numerical subjects through online mode:** In classroom teaching numerical subjects are taught on a blackboard/ whiteboard. In blackboard/ whiteboard the teacher can write the formula and methods to explain to students. Learners also can respond immediately to the teacher if there are any doubts about formulas and equations.

12. **Difficult to monitor discipline:**

The goal of teaching is to ensure that each student receives a quality education, skills and develops talent. In classroom teaching - the teacher ensures discipline is maintained properly, rules are enforced, and students are in a safe learning environment. But in the case of online classes teachers cannot exercise physical control on the learners.

13. **Research Issues for e-learning:** Current e-learning research brings together pedagogical, technical and organizational concerns within a wider set of socio-cultural factors. These factors influence the research agenda in the e-learning system. Understanding these broader social and cultural issues is of significant importance to the research communities involved in e-learning and will have a significant role in informing future practices.

Conclusion:

If the learners and teachers are blessed with requested gadgets Internet access and skills online education has the advantage of universal access to increase flexibility. It has also been observed that teachers were generally motivated when the wire provided with the opportunity 'to gain new pedagogical knowledge through online teaching, including the opportunity to experiment with new pedagogy, reflect on classroom teaching and gain a new understanding of assessment issues. E-Learning teaching may build confidence and communication skills in both to teacher and the thought, augment experimental learning, and allow wider choices gain knowledge.

Digital education code offering if mode a part of the institutional mission we thought planning for a reliable infrastructure and crystallized vision for learner support. But as far now keeping the challenges of E-Learning in mind, in a populous 8 technologies growing country like hours, blended learning scheme to be a most valuable option.

Except that, it must be said that today's 3G, 4G, 5G Internet facilities-based only video conferencing, classes have pacified this severity, still not be the best option of regular classes. So far out country India is concerned, big sectional of people from rural and labour classes, BPL (below poverty line), is still far away from the reaching of best Internet facilities, good Electricity connections. Therefore, E-Learning is still not fulfilling the desired inputs in our education system.

References:

- Rasmitadila, Aliyyah R. R., Rachmadtullah R., Samsudin A., Syaodih E., Nurtanto M., and Tambunan A. R. S. (2020). The Perceptions of Primary School Teachers of Online Learning during the COVID-19 Pandemic Period: A Case Study in Indonesia. *Journal of Ethnic and Cultural Studies*,Vol. 7, No. 2, pp. 90-109.
- Rapanta C., Botturi L., Goodyear P., Guardia L., and Koole M. (7 July 2020). Online University Teaching During and After the Covid-19 Crisis: Refocusing Teacher Presence and Learning Activity, *Postdigital Science and Education*. (2), pp. 923-945.
- Mathivanan S. K., Jayagopal P., Ahmed S., Manivannan S. S., Kumar P. J., Raja K. T., Dharinya S. S., and Prasad R. G., (24 February 2021). Adoption of E-Learning during Lockdown in India. *International Journal of System Assurance Engineering and Management*. pp. 10.
- Shea P. (January 2007). Bridges and Barriers to Teaching Online College Courses: A Study of Experienced Online Faculty in Thirty-six Colleges. *Journal of Asynchronous Learning Networks*. 11(2), pp. 73-128.
- AISHE Report 2018-19, Department of Higher Education MHRD, New Delhi.
- A Quick Evaluation Study of Anganwadis Under ICDS (June 2015). NITI AAYOG. Programme Evaluation Organization. Government of India. New Delhi-110001.
- World Inequality Database on Education from https://www.education-inequalities.org.

- O.V. Astafeva, E.P. Pecherskaya, T.M. Tarasova, E.V. Korobejnikova, Lecture Notes in
- Networks and Systems, 84, 382 (2020)
- O.V. Astafeva, National Interests: Priorities and Security, 15, 4, 772 (2019)
- A.P. Zhabin, S.A. Shchennikov, A.G. Abrosimov and others, Strategic educational
- alliances as a mechanism for transforming an innovative educational environment (2008)
- S.A. Shchennikov, Open distance education (2002)
- E.P. Pecherskaya, L.V. Averina, L.G. Karanatova, S.A. Kozhevnikova, The European
- Proceedings of Social & Behavioural Sciences EpSBS, 365 (2019)
- A.Sh. Kamaletdinov, A.A. Ksenofontov, Management sciences in the modern world.
- Collection of scientific conference reports, 279 (2019)
- Yu. Fukolova, Harvard Business Review, 96 (2018)

CHAPTER SIX

Covid-19 Vaccination Drive in India: Facilitation to Front Doorstep

------*Dr. Abhishek Srivastava*

Introduction

This covid pandemic has shown how healthcare system flaws can have serious consequences for public health, economic progress, government trust, and social cohesion. Since the pandemic's lethality was waning, the country was hit by a second wave last year. Throughout it all, the healthcare industry had to rise to the challenge with constant innovation, devising new ways to meet urgent needs and provide patient care. Consumers were quick to adopt digitised services, demonstrating a significant behavioural shift, as their reliance on healthcare services increased by a factor of ten. By developing new drugs, vaccines, and tests for covid, pharmaceutical research and development (R&D) exploded into life in unprecedented ways. Meanwhile, India has done a fantastic job automating the Covid Vaccination Drive, and in such a short period of time. Government machinery, with the help of IT industries, did their best to meet the demand of the hour! Market participants believe automation will be the next big thing in logistics as the country emerges from the pandemic and technology takes on a whole new meaning in this post-Covid world.

While the rapid development of COVID 19 vaccines is a remarkable achievement, vaccinating the entire world poses numerous challenges, from production to distribution, deployment, and, most importantly, acceptance. The ability of governments to communicate the benefits of vaccination and to deliver vaccines safely and effectively is critical to public confidence in vaccines. This brief discusses the role of governments in promoting trust in their ability to procure and distribute resources efficiently and equitably, as well as in their ability to communicate effectively about their effectiveness and safety. While only a small percentage of the population is anti-vaccination, there is apprehension about COVID 19 vaccination in many countries. Recognizing that the scale of vaccination campaigns required is unprecedented, government efforts to build trust will be critical to their success and the emergence of more resilient societies following the crisis.

Success Story of CoWIN Application

The Ministry of Health and Family Welfare of India owns and operates CoWIN (Covid Vaccine Intelligence Network), an Indian government web portal for COVID-19 vaccination registration. It shows available COVID-19 vaccine booking slots in the area and allows you to book them on the website. Vaccination slots can be booked on the same day or a few days ahead of time. The Aarogya Setu and UMANG Apps have also incorporated the platform. (The platform can also be used to obtain a certificate following COVID-19 vaccination.) In the country, three vaccines can currently be registered on the platform: Covishield, Covaxin, and Sputnik V.

Exclusive Features Offered by CoWIN App.

- Registration and booking of vaccination slots: For Co-Win, beneficiaries and officials involved in the vaccination process can use a mobile app and a website. By registering with their mobile number on Co-Win, one can book a vaccination slot. Prior registration on Cowin.gov.in is no longer required, but it is necessary to keep track of all vaccinations on this site.
- Download a certificate: Following immunisation, one can download a vaccination certificate from one's Co-Win account, which will become a vital travel document in the coming days. Other countries are expected to recognise the Co-Win certificate as genuine proof of immunisation, according to the Ministry of External Affairs.
- Vaccine certificate editing: Using the platform, any inaccuracies in the vaccine certificate can now be corrected.
- On the certificate, fill in the following information about your passport: The portal now allows users to link their passport to their Covid-19 immunisation certificate, making it easier for Indians who want to travel abroad.

- Combine the certificates: Beneficiaries who received two doses and two different certificates from two different phone lines can now combine the two certificates.

CoWIN TimeLine

- On January 16, 2021, CoWIN began vaccinating Frontline Workers in the country with COVID-19.
- On March 1, 2021, the platform began offering vaccination to all residents over 60, residents between 45 and 60 with one or more qualifying comorbidities, and any health care or frontline worker who did not receive a dose during phase 1.
- Beginning April 1, 2021, all residents over the age of 45 will be eligible. Registration for the next phase began on April 28, 2021, with all residents over the age of 18 becoming eligible on May 1, 2021.
- On June 28, 2021, it was announced that over 50 countries would receive an open source version.On 21 October 2021, according to the CoWin portal, India crosses 1 billion doses.
- According to the CoWin portal, India will reach 1 billion doses on October 21, 2021.
- Eligibility for teens aged 15 to 18 years old was extended on January 3, 2022, with registration beginning on January 1, 2022, on CoWIN.

A COVID booster dose drive for frontline workers, 60+ people with comorbidities, healthcare workers, and election workers began on January 10, 2022. They can either go to a vaccination centre or book a slot on the CoWIN Platform. The booster (precaution dose) will only be given with the same shots as before, and there should be a nine-to-twelve-month gap between the second and third shots.

"We have certainly created a scalable platform; despite such large numbers, there was not a single glitch, and I don't think there will be any if the numbers go up even more," says the team.

R S Sharma, Chief Executive of the National Health Authority

"The digital infrastructure developed by RS Sharma, CoWin, is incredible. My Seattle friend's vaccination certificate was scribbled on a scrap of paper. My vaccination certificate was sent digitally with a QR code, and I received it on my phone within 2 minutes of receiving it."

Infosys chairman Nandan Nilekani

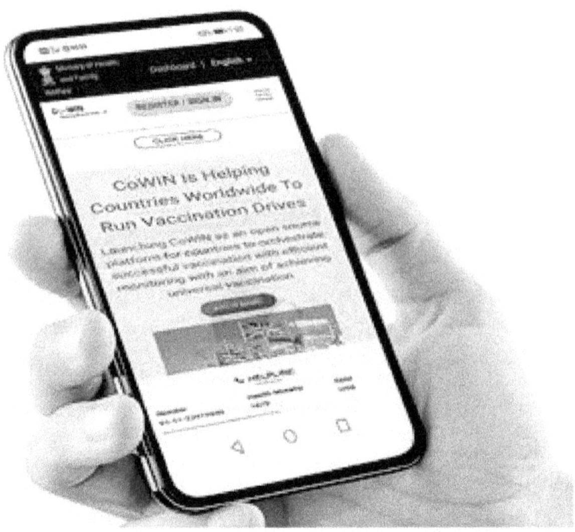

The cumulative COVID-19 vaccine doses administered in the country have reached 158.74 crore so far, the Union Health Ministry said on Tuesday, January 18, 2022

Digitalization of Vaccination through Co-WIN

The Co-WIN application is the vaccination drive's digital backbone, allowing citizens to register and schedule vaccination sessions online in the centres of their choice. The citizen self-registration module will ensure that only deserving candidates for vaccines are identified. Multiple roles can be created in the Co-WIN application for orchestrating vaccination drives at various levels.

In addition, the Government of India has launched a dashboard on state-by-state Covid-19 vaccination of citizens, which shows total vaccination doses, first and second doses, and states with the highest vaccination statistics, among other things.

Below mentioned charts are showing Registration Trends & Vaccination Trends of our Country

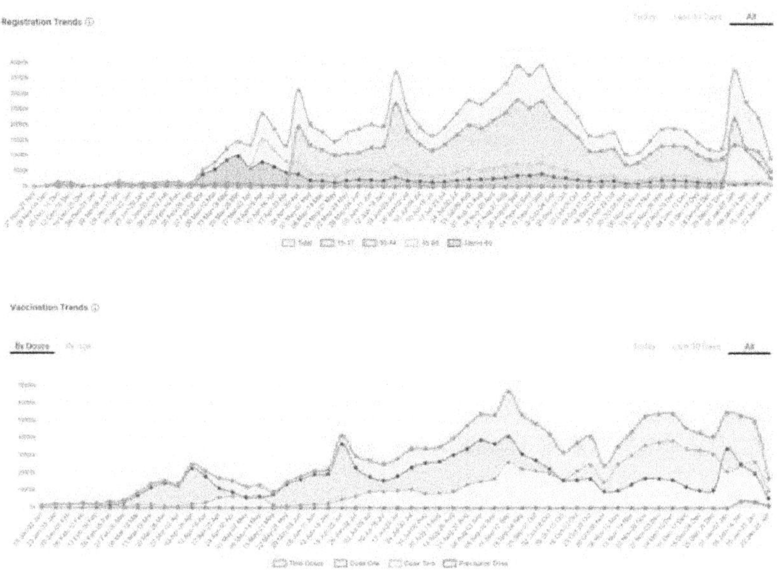

The government of India will inform states and union territories ahead of time about vaccine doses that will be delivered to them. Similarly, states/ UTs should allocate doses to districts and vaccination centres well in advance. They should also make the information about the above available to the public availability at the district and vaccination centre levels, as well as widespread distribution Its visibility and convenience among the local population are maximised citizens' participation.

Domestic vaccine manufacturers are given the option of providing vaccines directly to private hospitals in order to encourage vaccine production and encourage new vaccines. This would be limited to a quarter of their monthly output. The demand for private hospitals would be aggregated by states/UTs, with an equitable distribution of large and small private hospitals and regional balance in mind. The Government of India will facilitate the supply of these vaccines to private hospitals and their payment through the National Health Authority's electronic platform based on this aggregated demand.

This would allow smaller and more remote private hospitals to obtain vaccines on time, resulting in more equitable access and regional balance.

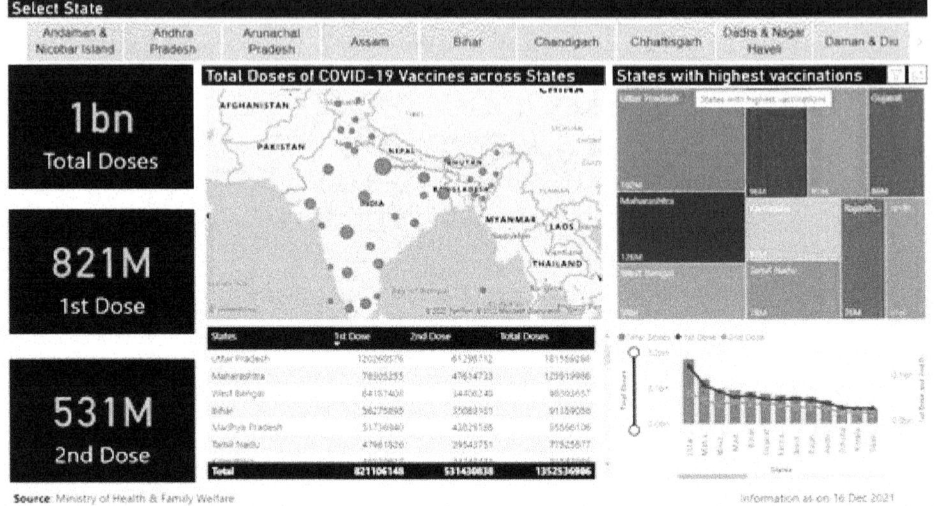

Dashboard on state-wise Covid-19 vaccination of citizens in India
https://dashboard.cowin.gov.in/

Conclusion

India has stood firm in the face of the unprecedented challenge posed by COVID-19 infections, with government and non-government support bolstering preventive and therapeutic healthcare facilities, diagnostic and research facilities, and tracking services to reduce human mortality. During these trying times, the national and state management models (including the largest state, Uttar Pradesh, with a population of 240 million) have been lauded nationally and internationally for planning and execution. The nation was caught off guard by the second wave's speed and magnitude. Despite this challenge, the case fatality rate has not yet reached the levels seen in many high-income countries that have the financial luxury of complete lockdowns for months at a time. Despite the virus's effects, India has remained resilient and has not seen a breakdown in the supply chain of health infrastructure. In this pandemic, India can also take pride in being a country that has treated its rich and poor equally. In retrospect, it's always easier to be wiser. For all decisions, history will be the judge and jury.

References:

- Pandey, A., Sah, P., Moghadas, S. M., Mandal, S., Banerjee, S., Hotez, P. J., & Galvani, A. P. (2021). Challenges facing COVID-19 vaccination in India: Lessons from the initial vaccine rollout. Journal of Global Health, 11.
- Prakash, S., & Gunalan, I. (2021, October). Developing Digital Governance for Managing the Challenges of the COVID-19 Pandemic-Case Study India. In 14th International Conference on Theory and Practice of Electronic Governance (pp. 541-543).
- Thakur, J. S., & Kaur, H. (2021). Vaccine distribution for COVID-19 and equity issues in India. International Journal of Noncommunicable Diseases, 6(5), 98.
- Choudhary, O. P., Choudhary, P., & Singh, I. (2021). India's COVID-19 vaccination drive: key challenges and resolutions. The Lancet Infectious Diseases, 21(11), 1483-1484.
- KARANDIKAR, T., PRABHU, A., MATHUR, M., ARORA, M., HEMANK, L., & KUMARAGURU, P. (2021). India's Vaccination Response to COVID-19.

CHAPTER SEVEN

Changing Attitudes Among Teenagers During And After Covid-19: An Analytical Study

-----**Prashanth Kumar H P***P. Horsley Solomon***Sayan Chakraborty

Introduction

Coronavirus is the largest form of RNA virus. It causes a respiratory infection that ranges from the common cold to various severe diseases. Today in the whole world coronavirus usually called covid-19 is a crucial topic for every human being. It's a very contagious viral disease that came over in December 2019 and the effects are continuously being spread worldwide. It was foremost discovered in the Wuhan district of China and the World Health Organization on 11th March of the year 2020 acknowledged the severity of the virus and announced it as a source of global pandemic (Corrigan, et. al, 2012). The studies have pointed out that older individuals are very prone to this disease although children have less risk here. But a new form of coronavirus is discovered in the meantime which is causing skin lesions. Children facing routine disruption these days for the closure of schools, colleges, universities. After all these the no of people started suffering from anxiety and psychiatric disorder due to not getting attached with the people during this pandemic situation. (Lee, et. al, 2022). Mostafavi (2021) published a poll in the Michigan Health Blog. The findings of the poll are discussed in Figure 1.

Figure 1 Effects of the Pandemic on Teen Mental Health

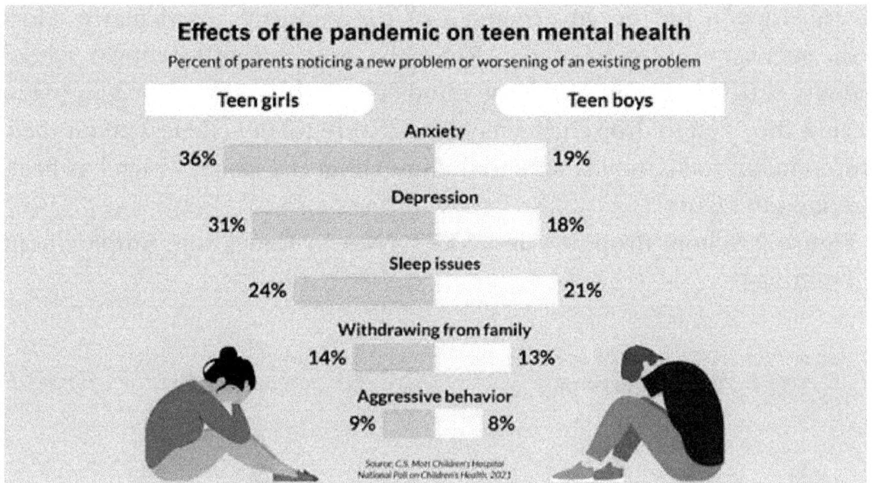

Source Mostafavi (2021)

Lockdown made pressure on teenagers not going outside regularly which includes closure of schools and colleges all over the world causing a negative impact on 91% of the world student population. This lockdown system has disrupted the education life, social life, and physical activities too. This has also led to a lack of creativity, innovations, boredom, and not following the routine. The teenagers and children have become more dependent on their parents, clingier, and seeking attention. The cancellation of exams, exchange programs, and academic events has made anxious behaviour for teenagers. It is also found that youth social distancing is a primary way to motivate society to be sincere in their lives. Due to staying at home the use of the internet has increased much more compulsively. Worst of all when the schools and colleges got closed the teenagers and children suffering from household abuse were not able to report violence against this which led to suicides. In India, the student population is 472 million among which 40 million students have a significant effect because they belong to a poor family and are facing inequality in this pandemic situation. They started working in fields, rural areas as servants, and more on. Many teenagers are infected outside their hometown they had to face quarantine separated from their parents and return home. In China this case is performed by several adults, children have been separated from each other and follow the strict quarantine. Every parent got their children in learning and follow the rules given by the governments of the countries particularly. Most of the teenagers were the school students. And during lockdown school students suffered the max. A large number of kids were under depression because they had to drop their schools and were totally clueless about their future. Indian today report explored more about the same, which has been presented in Figure 2.

Figure 2 School dropouts and NEET (Not in Education, Employment or Training)

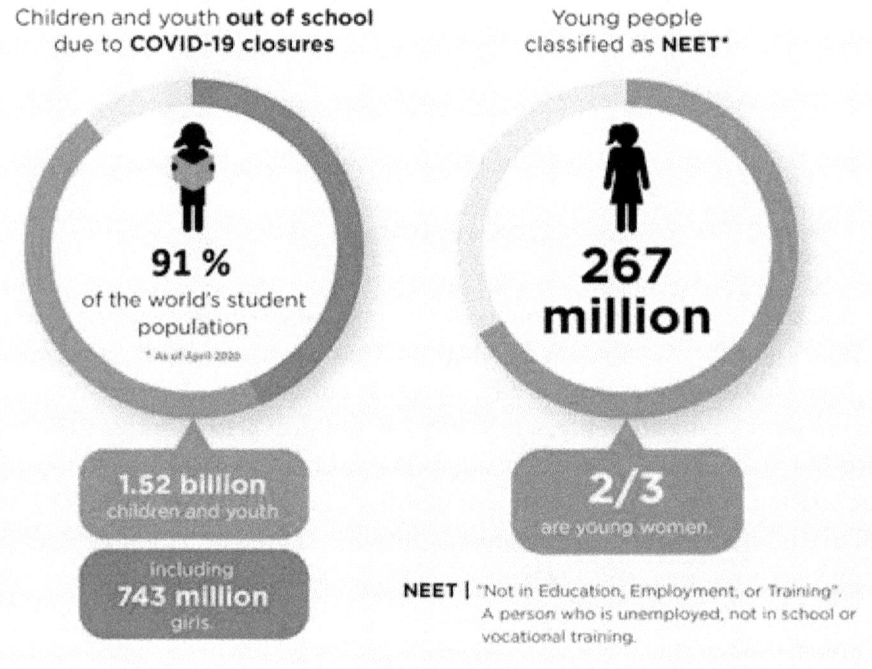

Source:United Nations

The pandemic has brought about a complex collection of issues ranging from uncertainty to social isolation, and parental angst that have had an impact on the mental health of children and adolescents. Today's need of teenagers is to be keeping the youth informed and up to date. They also need help teens cope with uncertaintyOffer relief from boredom. One also needs to be focus on athleticsand get youth input to problems and solve them together. There is also a room to address the financial concerns of the younger generations.

One of the most important things to make this feasible is to remember the basics and nature of the virus. "Google's DeepMind" and different AI techs have leaped forward with their knowledge of protein folding research to elucidate the protein morphology of viruses and make it open source.AI technology is being used to create drugs that fight the different hazardous diseases around the world, and when tissues first develop products based on infectious diseases, they are working to further try to treat the coronavirus increase. Within a few weeks of the epidemic, we used our investigative skills to recommend new drugs that could be beneficial. COVID19 is caused by a virus called SARSCoV2. It belongs to the coronavirus family and can range from common head and chest colds to more serious (but rare) illnesses such as "Severe Acute Respiratory Syndrome (SARS) and Middle Eastern Respiratory Syndrome (MERS)" contains a wide range of viruses that cause the disease. .. Like many other respiratory viruses, the coronavirus spreads rapidly through the droplets that erupt from the mouth and nose when breathing, coughing, sneezing, or speaking. COVID19 (Coronavirus Disease 2019) is an illness due to a virus infection called SARSCoV2, which was first identified in Wuhan, China in December 2019. It is highly contagious and is spreading rapidly throughout the world. COVID19 most commonly causes respiratory symbols and can feel like a cold, flu, or pneumonia. COVID19 can attack the lungs and respiratory system, as well as more. Other parts of your body can also be affected by the disease.

Literature Review

The virus has put billions of lives in terrific situations. People are breaking down physically, psychologically, and socially. Compared to SARS COVID has higher transmissibility, worst recovery, frequent mutations leading to uncontrollable situations. This disease not only infects the respiratory system but also goes on damaging the brain, liver, kidneys, and endocrine system with no curable options. There was a lack of emergency treatments has taken away many lives globally.

Most people with COVID 19 have mild symptoms, but some have a serious illness. Some people, including those with few or no symptoms, may have a post-COVID illness or "long COVID." Elderly people and people with certain underlying illnesses are at increased risk of serious illness due to

COVID 19. Hundreds of thousands of people have died of COVID 19 in the United States. Vaccines against COVID 19 are safe and effective. The vaccine teaches the immune system to fight the virus that causes COVID19. Covid-19 has a multi-factorial impact on the children and teenager population, social isolation can trigger, Health policies (Oosterhoff & Palmer, 2020).

The "World Health Organization" has acknowledged coronavirus disease as a pandemic-causing virus in 2019. Global adjustments have been discontinued to prevent the spread of the virus. Pandemics are now defined as situations where a wide range of people are suffering from the same fears, affecting most of the world's population. Symptoms of the coronavirus include respiratory infections, fever and cough, shortness of breath, shortness of breath, tiredness, and sore throat. It also causes new dysphasia, chest compressions, bluish lips, and face. During this pandemic, three groups of people are still at high risk: elderly people over 70 years old, people with chronic illnesses such as diabetes, cancer, high blood pressure, liver disease, cardiovascular disease, and respiratory illness, and physically inactive people (Jiang, et. al, 2021).

Visitors returning home should nod or keep a distance of at least 1 meter and remain in Quarantine for a minimum of 15 days. The family should actually wash their hands while they are together and also disinfect homes, especially places that people often touch. Keep a little distance for those who are not good at staying at home. Seek medical attention immediately if you experience any symptoms. When you are in a public place, follow the same rules as at home. And most importantly, look forward to this situation.

During the situation of covid-19 children and teenagers as well appear to less risked people in this situation. But this pandemic situation has created problems in other ways. The first precaution for these people was to close all the school's high school's colleges and universities all over the world, which lead to being indoors with parents and not seeing close friends and other people. The people who are just crossing the childhood stage to become an adult need proper education and different development needs to be an adult. Now the main factor is social media where teenagers invest their time In a whole day by which they are getting distant from parents. It is a very hard time for a teenager to develop themselves to be good adults (Esposito, et. al, 2022).

Teenagers meanwhile are taught the rules and regulations to be safe and keep the family members safe at the same time. They are said to perform some concrete steps to avoid getting infected, and also not let the loved ones do so. Life has changed so much then the daily routine has also changed widely. Teenagers depend on their mobile phones to connect with their friends and close ones, so the parents need to provide them the facilities rather than simply limiting the use of the internet (Hoffmann, et. al, 2021).

The impact of pandemics on young people is instantly serious. Discuss special things like proms, spending time with friends, going to concerts and more. Now, these things are avoided in this situation leading to distress circumstances, and the results will turn into deeper and long-term consequences. Here it also includes family wellbeing, educational future, and aesthetic participation (Ndulue, & Orji, 2021).

The largest hazard of the coronavirus is the extent of dissemination. Policymakers are introducing measures like quarantines round as a measure to break the chain of spread in the sector due to the fact they can`t thoroughly reveal neighbourhood outbreaks. One of the handiest measures to become aware of sick sufferers thru the observation of CCTV photographs which are nonetheless around us and to discover and separate people who have severe symptoms of the disorder and who've been in contact and sterilized the associated surfaces. Smart device packages are frequently used to preserve an eye fixed on people`s sports and to evaluate whether or not or now no longer they have got are available in contact with an inflamed human. Identification of the infected from the huge population and preventing the transmission of pathogens, they want to expand the reach of vaccinations on a scale to reach herd immunity (Dondi, A., 2021).

According to a study by "the Centres for Disease Control and Prevention (CDC)", teenage suicide attempts increased dramatically during the blockade of Covid 19 in 2020 and 2021. In addition, boys of the same age group also had a 4% increase in suicide attempts. More children were at risk of abuse and negligence at home as the Covid19 or coronavirus pandemic kept children and their families indoors during periods of self-isolation (Lee, et. al, 2021).

People experience a wide multiplicity of new or persistent symptoms that can last for weeks or months after being first infected with the virus that causes COVID19. Unlike other types of post-COVID illnesses of type, which tend to occur only in people with severe illness, those infected with COVID 19 are mildly ill but initially asymptomatic (Zahrin, et. al, 2021). These symptoms can also occur. .. People generally report different combinations of the following symptoms:

Dyspnoea or shortness of breath, fatigue or malaise, symptoms that worsen after physical or mental activity (also known as post-abnormal fatigue), difficulty thinking or concentrating (sometimes called "brain fog"), Cough, chest or abdominal pain, headache, fast heartbeat or throbbing heart (also known as palpitation), joint or muscle pain, pins and needles, diarrhea, dyspnoea, fever, dizziness when standing up (light-headedness), With skin rashes, mood changes, odor and taste changes, and changes in the menstrual cycle(Jain, et. al, 2020).

Conclusion

So as a final point there has been drastic push in teenager's behaviour due to pandemic induced by covid-19. There are few ways by which teenagers can be helped in this pandemic situation are: Working together to create a new normal life despite struggling with this situation by sticking to the schedule, conversation time for the home members, and by taking some personal space or we can say it alone time in the home. Communicate honestly and openly with the teenagers and make them understand that it is not the right time to communicate with people outside socially, and share information about what is happening outside the worldwide pandemic. Help them do the plans and recover them from the past situations which can lead to suicidal attempts and can bring mental disorder or disruption. Stay safely connected through the virtual world like Facebook, WhatsApp, whatever the virtual apps are there to make new friend maybe. Bring a sense of responsibility for the family members and help them too to connect with their close ones through the virtual world (Lessard, & Puhl, 2021).

References

- Oosterhoff, B., & Palmer, C. A. (2020). Attitudes and psychological factors associated with news monitoring, social distancing, disinfecting, and hoarding behaviors among US adolescents during the coronavirus disease 2019 pandemic. *JAMA pediatrics, 174*(12), 1184-1190.
- Lee, O., Park, S., Kim, Y., & So, W. Y. (2022, January). Participation in Sports Activities before and after the Outbreak of COVID-19: Analysis of Data from the 2020 Korea National Sports Participation Survey. In *Healthcare* (Vol. 10, No. 1, p. 122). Multidisciplinary Digital Publishing Institute.
- Jiang, R., Shao, B., Si, S., Sato, R., & Tsuneo, J. (2021). Health Communication in Games at the Early Stage of COVID-19 Epidemic: A Grounded Theory Study Based on Plague, Inc. *Games for Health Journal,*

10(6), 408-419.

- Corrigan, P. W., Morris, S. B., Michaels, P. J., Rafacz, J. D., & Rüsch, N. (2012). Challenging the public stigma of mental illness: a meta-analysis of outcome studies. *Psychiatric Services, 63*(10), 963-973.
- Dondi, A., Candela, E., Morigi, F., Lenzi, J., Pierantoni, L., & Lanari, M. (2021). Parents' perception of food insecurity and its effects on their children in Italy six months after the COVID-19 pandemic outbreak. *Nutrients, 13*(1), 121.
- Esposito, C., Di Napoli, I., Agueli, B., Marino, L., Procentese, F., & Arcidiacono, C. (2022). Well-Being and the COVID-19 Pandemic. *European Psychologist*.
- Hoffmann, A., Nanaki, E., Enevoldsen, P., & Xydis, G. (2021). A behavioral change study in Denmark engaging car drivers in reducing fuel consumption: The key is in the message. *International Journal of Sustainable Transportation*, 1-10.
- Ndulue, C., & Orji, R. (2021, June). Gender and the Effectiveness of a Persuasive Game for Disease Awareness Targeted at the African Audience. In *Adjunct Proceedings of the 29th ACM Conference on User Modeling, Adaptation and Personalization* (pp. 318-324).
- Lee, J., Lim, H., Allen, J., & Choi, G. (2021). Effects of Learning Attitudes and COVID-19 Risk Perception on Poor Academic Performance among Middle School Students. *Sustainability, 13*(10), 5541.
- Jain, O., Gupta, M., Satam, S., & Panda, S. (2020). Has the COVID-19 pandemic affected the susceptibility to cyberbullying in India?. *Computers in Human Behavior Reports, 2*, 100029.
- Lessard, L. M., & Puhl, R. M. (2021). Adolescent academic worries amid COVID-19 and perspectives on pandemic-related changes in teacher and peer relations. *School Psychology*.
- Zahrin, S. N. A., Sawai, R. P., Sawai, J. P., Ab Rahman, Z., & Samsudin, M. Z. (2021). EMOTION, MENTAL AND SPIRITUAL REGULATION OF THE HIGHER EDUCATION COMMUNITY DURING THE COVID-19 PANDEMIC. *ASEAN Journal of Teaching & Learning in Higher Education, 13*(2).
- Mostafavi (2021) Children's Health, National Poll: Pandemic Negatively Impacted Teens' Mental Health, Michigan Mental Health, March 15, 2021, Retrieved from https://healthblog.uofmhealth.org/childrens-health/national-poll-pandemic-negatively-impacted-teens-mental-health on 22-01-2022, at 10:10.

- Kannan, S. (2020), Covid stress is catching them young, Deep Dive, India Today, Singapore, December 26, 2020, Retrieved from https://www.indiatoday.in/coronavirus-outbreak/story/deep-dive-covid-stress-is-catching-them-young-1753170-2020-12-25 on 22-01-2022, at 10:20.
- https://healthblog.uofmhealth.org/

CHAPTER EIGHT

"2020:Covid–19 Hits The Education System"

------*Pradip Das*

Introduction :

Online Educational system is a tool which helps making the teaching–learning process more user-friendly, more innovative, more creative and even more flexible. Online learning is defined as “learning experiences in synchronous or asynchronous environments using different devices (e.g., mobile phones, laptops, etc.) with internet access. In these environments, students can be anywhere (independent) to learn and interact with instructors and other students” (Singh & Thurman, 2019). The systematic learning environment is structured in the sense that students attend live lectures, there are real-time classroom interactions between teachers and learners, and there is a chance of instant feedback, whereas non-systematic learning environments are not properly structured. In the second type of learning environment, learning content is not available in the form of live lectures or classes; it is available at different learning systems and forums. All the educational institutions like schools, colleges, and universities in India are generally based only on age old traditional methods of teaching-learning, that is, lectures in face-to-face mode in a classroom. Though some academic units have started following blended learning, still a lot of them are engaged with old method of teaching. The sudden outbreak of a deadly disease called Covid-19 caused by a Corona Virus (SARS-CoV-2) shook the utmost world. The World Health Organization declared this as a pandemic. This transformed situation challenged the whole education system across the world and forced the educators to shift to an online mode of teaching overnight. Most of the educational institutions those were earlier stubborn to stick only on traditional pedagogical approach had no option but to shift entirely to online teaching–learning.

Review of Related Literature on the impact of Online Education system During Covid-19 Situation

Knowledge delivery becomes more challenging with the rise of natural disasters like floods, cyclones, earthquakes, hurricanes day by day. These hazards close the doors of schools, colleges and universities in several ways. Sometimes, it creates serious consequences for students and deprives them of their fundamental right to education and poses them to future risk. "100 million children and young people are affected by natural disasters every year. Most of them face disruption to their schooling" (World Vision). Situations of crisis and conflicts are the biggest hurdles in the way to education. Many students and teachers also face psychological problems during these crisis situations—some are stress, fear, anxiety, depression, and insomnia that lead to a lack of focus and concentration.

Disasters create havoc in the lives of people (Di Pietro, 2017). With the global hike in temperatures and changing weather patterns, the numbers of extreme weather events have been increased now-a-days causing varying amounts of loss to life and property. A large number of educational institutions were destroyed and thousands of students were affected by these natural disasters. They forced to stop their study in the midway. "Disruption of education can leave children at risk of child labor, early marriage, exploitation, and recruitment into armed forces" (Baytiyeh, 2018). When disasters and crises (man-made and natural) occur, schools and colleges need to be resilient and should find new ways to continue with teaching– learning activities (Chang-Richards et al., 2013). For example, in 2016, Italy experienced three violent and powerful earthquakes bringing huge devastation in the number of areas. About 1,00,000 people became homeless, buildings and structures collapsed with severe loss of life and property. The University of Camerino, one of the oldest universities in the world suffered an innumerable loss. The university was in huge problem , its structure collapsed, a large number of students became homeless and some flown away. In such crisis situations, students were in shortage of education and learning. It is correctly said, "It is difficult to stick to the traditional road when the road itself has crumbled." This means that instructions in face-to-face were not at all possible at that time; therefore, administration came forward to devise few plans to continue the educational processes. Before the devastating earthquake, learning in online version at the University was cumbersome. But they were unstoppable, and to carry on the teaching–learning processes smoothly, they used WebEx (an online tool) by Cisco. Webex helped professors in designing the instructional programs and sharing notes and presentations with students according to their need. Unbelievably, within a month, the university was well-versed with e-learning strategies and techniques.

They settled themselves comprehensively well in an e-learning world. They believed that, of course, the value of the face-toface instruction method should not be reduced, but e-learning can be used in a blended mode to bring in efficiency, effectiveness, and competitive edge over other competitors by imparting quality education (Barboni, 2019). In February 2011, Christchurch was shocked due to a 6.3 magnitude earthquake and the University of Canterbury collapsed. IT enabled education and online learning helped the university to begin again its operations and gave them a second chance to survive (Todorova & Bjorn-Andersen, 2011). At New Orleans, Southern University converted itself into an e-learning campus after the attack of violent hurricane. Several online courses were offered and mobiles were used to provide education to the displaced students (Omar et al., 2008

The Present scenario

The dangerous infectious disease Covid-19, due to Corona Virus, has severely affected the global financial market. This tragedy has also shocked the education sector globally. The Covid-19 pandemic outbreak forced many schools and colleges to remain closed temporarily for indefinite days. Almost every place is affected worldwide and there is a fear of losing this whole ongoing semester or even the upcoming semesters. Various schools, colleges, and universities had to stop face-to-face mode of teaching-learning. As per the outcome of the researches, it is uncertain to get back to normal teaching anytime soon. As social distancing is a must criterion at this stage, this will have disruptive effects on learning opportunities. Educational institutions are struggling to find solutions to this challenging situation. These circumstances make us realize that an urgent shift in planning is needed for academic institutions (Rieley, 2020). This is a situation that demands togetherness and humanity.

The need was urgent to protect and save our students, faculty, academic staff, communities, societies, and the nation as a whole. There are several arguments are associated with online pedagogy like accessibility, affordability, flexibility, learning pedagogy, life-long learning, and policy. It is said that online mode of learning is quite easy accessible and can even reach to rural and remote areas. It is considered to be a relatively less expensive mode of education in terms of the lower cost of transportation, accommodation, and the overall cost of institution-based learning.

Flexibility is another interesting factor of online learning; a learner can plan according to their time schedule. Combining face-to-face lectures with technology gives rise to blended learning and flipped classrooms; this type of learning environment can fasten the learning potential of the students. Students can learn as per their time and place, thereby life-long learning became an inevitable approach of life. The government also started recognizing the increasing importance of online learning in this dynamic world. The severe explosion of Corona Virus disease can make us add one more argument in terms of online learning, that is, whether it is the only solution during COVID – 19 Pandemic.

Objectives of the Study

1. To explore the growth and development of online learning in past and present context.

2. To conduct a Strengths, Weaknesses, Opportunities, & Challenges (SWOC) analysis of online learning during the Corona Virus pandemic.

3. To give some suggestions and recommendations for the success of the online mode of learning during a crisis-like situation like the Covid-19 Pandemic.

Research Methodology

It is a descriptive study and tries to understand the significance of e-learning during the crisis period and pandemics such as the Covid-19. The problems associated with online learning and probable solutions were also identified based on previous studies. The SWOC analysis was conducted to understand various strengths, weaknesses, opportunities, and challenges associated with online learning during this critical situation Content analysis was done for the research tool. The research method is descriptive research. The qualitative aspects of the research study were also taken into consideration. This study is completely based on secondary data. A systematic review was done in detail for the collected literature. Secondary sources of data used are

(a) journals,

(b) reports,

(c) documents,

(d) company websites and scholarly articles,

(e) research papers, and other academic publications.

History of Online Education System:

The 21st century has brought about a massive change in the world of education. Gone are those days when teaching was limited only within the confines of a classroom. The internet has brought about a paradigm shift in the fundamental way in which learning is done. It has taken learning beyond the hallowed walls of the universities and into the palms of everyone. But how did this radical transformation occur? though there are numerous examples of the usage of machines and tools in education throughout history, elearning in the modern sense of the term is a relatively new concept. Slide projectors and television-based classes have been in use since the 1950s. However, one of the first instances of online learning in the world can be traced back to 1960, at the University of Illinois, USA. Though the internet wasn't invented back then, students began learning from computer terminals that were interlinked to form a network. The first MAC in the 1980s enabled individuals to have computers in their homes, making it quite easier for them to learn about particular subjects and develop certain skill sets. Then, in the next decade, virtual learning environments came into existence truly, with people gaining access to a world of online information and e-learning opportunities. The first-ever completely online course was offered in 1984 by the University of Toronto. In 1986, the Electronic University Network was established for being used in DOS and Commodore 64 computers.

Three years later, the University of Phoenix became the first educational institution in the world to launch a wholly online collegiate institution, offering both bachelor's and master's degrees. This was the beginning of a revolution whose potential was largely unknown to the public back then, but one that would make learning greatly accessible and within reach of what people could ever have imagined. The Open University in Britain was one of the first universities in the world to begin online distance learning, in the early 1990s. Currently, the Indira Gandhi National Open University in India is the largest university in the world with around 4 million students enrolled, most of whom currently receive education via online methods. By the early 90s, very few schools had been set up that started delivering courses online only, making the most of the internet and bringing education to help those people who could not attend a college due to geographical or time constraints. Technological advancements also helped educational establishments to lessen the costs of distance learning, thus, helping bring education to a larger audience. New and experienced workers alike now had the opportunity to improve upon their industry-related knowledge and improve their skills. Thus, the individuals were enabled to access to earn online degrees and enrich their lives through expanded knowledge of the internet and online learning. The end of 2000 was inspired by flash video and mobile web. 2010 brought a massive change in online education. Social media, various websites, and YouTube came into popularity and became very popular. MOOC courses brought a revolutionary change in the education system. Interested learners can take the full opportunity of these online courses since then.

The Online Market Size: The Present Scenario Online learning is booming in current times. Aided by the widespread availability of high-speed internet, making use of new technologies such as 4G and the soon-to-be-released 5G, online learning is expected to grow by leaps and bounds in the foreseeable future. The worldwide market size of online learning is approximately $187.87 billion in 2019, a 400% increase over what it was just six years ago. This phenomenal growth has been made possible not just by the rapidly evolving scenario in the world of technology, but also by the spread of education in the developing world. Experts predict that the next wave of online education will occur not in North America and Europe, but in newly emerging markets like Africa, India, and China. Online learning is no longer just limited to colleges and universities. Right since primary school, online learning is gradually being incorporated into the curriculum.

The recent COVID-19 pandemic further illustrates the importance of online learning in today's school system, as it has proven to be a boon to both students and teachers alike who are unable to attend school due to the risk of disease spread. Beyond high school, online learning is steadily increasing its market share at the pre-university level. Furthermore, e-learning is expanding in presence beyond the traditional fields as:

Present Developments in Online Teaching-Learning Process:

Online learning has evolved far beyond its original capabilities. It is no longer limited to a didactic method, which had a one-way monologue from the teacher to the student. Current advances in online learning enable the student to play an active role in the learning process, with regular feedback and assessments. This has greatly improved the effectiveness of the teaching system, bringing it on par with classroom-based learning. Some of the features that give an edge to online education are:

Less expensive than traditional teaching methods: As the cost of teaching is low, the expenses borne by the students inevitably come down. This makes education far more widespread and economical.

Vast variety of available courses: These days, online courses on everything are available at the touch of a button – from religion to commerce, philosophy to fashion designing, programming to painting, photography to yoga – there is hardly any field that hasn't been touched by e-learning.

Study groups: There is a scope of engaging with like-minded students across the world, sharing information and ideas.

Flexibility: This can be in terms of time, money, and location. Online learning enables the student and the teacher to be present at opposite ends of the world, in different time zones, and yet have the knowledge imparted effectively.

Much less infrastructure required: This is a huge incentive to the education providers, as the additional costs are largely minimized.

Standardized quality: Since the content available online can be evaluated and revised at any point in time, it helps maintain a reasonable standard of quality.

Smartphones have played a crucial role in making online learning viable. It is rapidly gaining ground even in rural areas, bringing high-quality education, at par with the best in the world, available to the masses. Massive open online courses (known as MOOCs) are a promising new field. The New York Times had declared 2012 as "the year of the MOOC", and there has been no stopping since then. The total number of students enrolled in MOOCs has risen to about 100 million now. Thus, the recent developments in online learning can be broadly attributed to the following factors:

i) Innovation in smartphone technology

ii) High-speed data access

iii) Interactive learning models

iv) Rising number of startups in the e-learning field

SWOC Analysis of Online Learning: During Covid-19 situation:

The most recent dangerous disaster, in the form of the Covid-19, confined the world into their room. Almost all the schools, colleges, and universities are facing lockdowns in the worst affected areas to curb the further spread of the Corona Virus. Most of the academic institutions are, therefore, seeking the help of online education for the smooth conduct of teaching-learning. The SWOC Analysis of Online Learning is discussed below. In the last few years, e-learning has started gaining popularity in developing countries including India. Many platforms provide affordable courses to students via (MOOC) Massive Open Online Courses. Still, a lot of institutions in India were reluctant toward online teaching and learning. Anyway, the challenges posed by the Corona Virus pandemic introduced everyone to a new arena of online learning and remote teaching. Instructors indulged them in remote teaching via a few flat forms such as Google Hangouts, Skype, Adobe Connect, Microsoft teams, and a few more, though ZOOM emerged as a clear winner. Also, to conduct smooth teaching-learning programs, a list of online etiquettes was shared with students and proper instructions for attending classes were given to them (Saxena, 2020).

Strengths:

E-learning approaches and processes have really strengths. The online learning modes have the capacity to rescue us from these hard times. It is user-friendly and very flexible in time and location. The e-learning mode enables us to customize our procedures and processes based on the needs of the learners. There are an ample number of online tools that are important for an effective and efficient learning environment. Educators may use a combo of audio, videos, and text to reach out to their students in this pandemic time to maintain a live touch to their lectures. This can help in creating a collaborative and interactive learning environment where students can easily give their immediate feedback, ask questions, and learn with interest. The time and location-flexible feature of e-learning is effective during the pandemic times, such as Covid-19. As the closure of places and unsafe traveling by roads can create a lot of troubles, e-learning can remain one of the important options of getting an education at our homes or workplaces. Technology provides innovative and resilient solutions at times of pandemic situations to continue education and to help people to communicate and work in a virtual mode without the need for face-to-face mode. This leads to many system changes in organizations as they adopt new technology for interacting and working (Mark & Semaan, 2008).

Weaknesses:

Online Education has certain weaknesses in the form that it hampers the regular communication between the learner and the educator, leading to loss of human touch. Users can face many technical hindrances that slow down the teaching-learning process (Favalee al., 2020). Though the flexibility of time and location is one of the strengths of online learning, these aspects are fragile and create problems. Students' non-serious behavior creates a lot of problems. Though all the learners are not the same, they vary according to their capabilities and confidence level. Some do not feel the same comfortable while learning online which increases their frustration and confusion. Often this online education fails to understand the psychology of the students and utterly failed to reach them and inadequate customization of learning processes can obstruct the teaching process and create an imbalance.

Opportunities :

E-learning actually has a lot of opportunities available but this time of pandemic will allow online learning to boom as most academic institutions have switched to this mode of learning. Online Learning, Remote Working, and e-collaborations exploded during the outbreak of the Corona Virus crisis (Favale et al., 2020). Now, academic institutions can continue with this opportunity by making their teachers teach and students learn via different online approaches. The people are generally complacent and scared to try some new modes of learning. This crisis will be a new phase for e-learning and will allow people to look at the effective side of online learning technologies. The time is already started when there is a lot of scope in bringing out surprising innovations and digital technologies. Already, EdTech companies are doing well by helping us fight the pandemic and not letting learning to be stopped. Teachers can practice technology and can design various flexible programs for students' better comprehension. The usage of online learning will test both the educator and learners. It will enhance problem-solving skills, critical thinking skills, analytical abilities, and adaptability among the students. In this crucial situation, any age group learners can access the online tools and get the benefits of time and location flexibility associated with e-learning. Teachers can develop innovative pedagogical methodologies in this panicky situation, termed as Panicgogy. EdTech startups have plenty of opportunities to bring about radical changes in nearly all the aspects associated with education ranging from, teaching, learning, evaluation, assessment, results, certification, degrees, and so on. Also, increasing market demand for online learning is an amazing opportunity for EdTech start-ups to bring technological disruption in the education sector.

Challenges:

Online learning faces a number of challenges ranging from learners' issues, teachers' issues, content issues, and pedagogical issues. It is a challenge for institutions to engage students and make them participate in the teaching-learning process for the whole pandemic time.

It is a challenge for teachers to transfer from offline mode to online mode, changing their teaching pedagogies and managing their time. It is challenging to develop content which not only covers the curriculum but also engages the students (Kebritchi et al., 2017). The quality of e-Learning programs is truly a challenge. There is no clear stipulation by the government in their educational policies about e-learning programs.

There is a lack of standards for quality, quality control, development of e-resources, and e-content delivery. This problem needs to be solved immediately so that everyone can enjoy the benefits of quality education via e-learning (Cojocariu et al., 2014). One should not merely focus on the pros attached to the adoption of online learning during crises but should also take account of developing and enhancing the quality of virtual courses delivered in such emergencies (Affouneh et al., 2020).

A lot of time and cost is involved in e-learning. A considerable amount of investment is needed for getting the devices and equipment, maintaining the equipment, training the human resources, and developing the online content. Therefore, an effective and efficient educational system needs to be developed to impart education via online mode. Ensuring digital equity is crucial in this tough time.

Not all the teachers, as well as students, have equal access to all digital devices, the internet, and Wi-Fi. Unavailability of proper digital tools, no internet connections, or interrupted Wi-Fi services can cause a lot of trouble due to which many students might lose out on learning opportunities. Efforts should be taken by institutions to ensure that every student and faculty is having proper and equal access to the required resources. They must also ensure that all the educational apps work on mobile phones as well, in case students do not have laptops. Therefore, steps must be taken to reduce the gap of the digital divide.

Findings:

According to World Economic Forum, the Covid-19 pandemic also has changed the way how several people receive and impart education. To find new solutions for our recent problems, we ought to bring in some much-demanded innovations and change. Teachers, as well as students, have become habitual to traditional methods of teaching-learning in the form of face-to-face lectures, and therefore, they are not ready to accept any change. But amidst this pandemic situation, we have no other alternative left other than adapting to the dynamic system and accepting the change. It will be beneficial for the academic sector and could bring a large number of surprising innovations. But amidst all, we cannot neglect and forget the students with limited access to all online technology.

These students may lose out when classes occur online due to their restricted financial resources. This is all because of the heavy costs associated with digital devices and internet data plans. This digital divide often widens the gaps of inequality. This terrible time of fate has taught us many new things. Everything is so unpredictable that we should be prepared to face challenges. Though this COVID-19 outbreak did not give us much time to plan we should take a lesson from which that planning is the key. We should plan everything, no matter if plan A fails, plan B must be ready. We have to do scenario planning for that. We have to be prepared for all types of critical and challenging situations which may occur and plan accordingly.

This pandemic has also taught us that students must acquire certain skills like problem-solving, critical thinking, and most importantly adaptability to survive the crisis. Educational institutions should build resilience in their systems to ensure and prioritize the presence of these skills in their students. "The key lesson for others may be to embrace e-learning technology before disaster strikes!" (Todorova & BjornAndersen, 2011). Today, we are compelled to learn online mode of education., it would be surely easier for us if we have already mastered it. The time we engaged in learning the modes could have been spent on nurturing innovative content. But it is better late than never. COVID-19 pandemic surely has speed up the process of online learning.

For instance, e-application like ZOOM, Google Meet, CISCO WEBEX allow conducting live online classes, web-conferencing, webinars, video chats, and live meetings. In this crisis period when most of the Secondary schools are closed due to lockdowns/curfews and most of the people are working from home, these apps helped in keeping people connected via video conferencing. Disasters will continue to occur and technologies will likely help us cope with them (Meyer & Wilson, 2011). Don Dippo, The Co-Principal Investigator at the Borderless Higher education for Refugees said that "We are in a world where conflict and environmental destruction ... are going to have lots of people, families, and communities, living in precarious contexts.

The willingness of post-secondary institutions to step up and engage and provide opportunities for those people will never be as large as the need. The only way we can even make a dent in this is to learn to collaborate and cooperate across institutions and across time and spatial boundaries. The only way really to do that is to rely on technology to create conditions to allow people to collaborate." We should be more adaptive to accept changes need in the environment and can adjust ourselves to different delivery modes, for instance, remote learning or online learning in situations of pandemics such as Covid-19.

Institutions and organizations should be prepared to deal with challenges such as pandemics and natural disasters (Seville et al., 2012). Reliability and sufficient availability of Information Communication Technology infrastructure, learning tools, digital learning resources in the form of Massive Open Online Courses, e-books, e-notes, and so on are of utmost importance in such severe situations (Huang et al., 2020). Instruction, content, motivation, relationships, and mental health are the five important things that an educator must keep in mind while imparting online education (Martin, 2020). Some teaching strategies (lectures, case-study, debates, discussions, experiential learning, brainstorming sessions, games, drills, etc.) can be used online to facilitate effective and efficient teaching and learning practices. In such panicky situations, teaching and learning should be made interesting to reduce the stress, fear, and anxiety levels of people.

Conclusion:

Students and teachers across various universities have never practiced e-learning in reality. Most of them are comfortable with traditional modes of teaching. The COVID-19 outbreak is the opportunity to make out the best from the current situation. We are learning a lot in this challenging situation. Amidst a lot of tools available, teachers are required to choose the best tool and implement it to impart education to their students. Step-bystep guidance is required and academic institutions can guide the teachers and students on how to access and use various e-learning tools and how to cover a major part of curriculum content via these technologies thereby reducing digital illiteracy. Teachers can present the curriculum through a number of formats, like, videos, audios, and texts. It is beneficial if educators complement their lectures with video chats, virtual meetings, and so on to get immediate feedback and maintain a human touch with the students. Disasters and pandemic such as Covid-19 has already created a lot of chaos and tensions; therefore, there is an important need to study and apply the technology deeply and with due diligence to balance these fears and tensions amidst such crisis

References:-

- Affouneh, S., Salha, S., N., Khlaif, Z. (2020). Designing quality e-learning environments for emergency remote teaching in coronavirus crisis. Interdisciplinary Journal of Virtual Learning in Medical Sciences, 11(2),1–3. Google Scholar
- Barboni, L. (2019). From shifting earth to shifting paradigms: How webex helped our university overcome an earthquake. CISCO, Upshot By Influitive. Google Scholar
- Baytiyeh, H. (2018). Online learning during post-earthquake school closures", Disaster Prevention and Management. An International Journal, 27(2), 215– 227. https://doi.org/10.1108/DPM-07-2017-0173 Google Scholar
- Chang-Richards, A., Vargo, J., Seville, E. (2013). Organisational resilience to natural disasters: New Zealand's experience (English translation). China Policy Review, 10, 117–119. Google Scholar
- Cojocariu, V.-M., Lazar, I., Nedeff, V., Lazar, G. (2014). SWOT analysis of e-learning educational services from the perspective of their beneficiaries. Procedia-Social and Behavioral Sciences, 116, 1999–2003. Google Scholar |
- Crossref Di Pietro, G. (2017). The academic impact of natural disasters: Evidence from the L'Aquila earthquake. Education Economics, 26(1), 62– 77. https://doi.org/10.1080/09645292.2017.1394984 Google Scholar | Crossref
- Favale, T., Soro, F., Trevisan, M., Drago, I., Mellia, M. (2020). Campus traffic and e-Learning during COVID-19 pandemic. Computer Networks, 176, 107290. Google Scholar | Crossref
- Huang, R. H., Liu, D. J., Tlili, A., Yang, J. F., Wang, H. H., Zhang, M., Lu, H., Gao, B., Cai, Z., Liu, M., Cheng, W., Cheng, Q., Yin, X., Zhuang, R., Berrada, K., Burgos, D., Chan,

CHAPTER NINE

COVID-19 Vaccine Diplomacy in the Indo-Pacific Region

-----***Mr. UdayModak***

1.0 Introduction:

When the Covid 19 epidemic spread from country to country, from continent to continent. The virus has had a devastating effect on the world economy. There is no doubt that the nations of the first world were not spared from this epidemic. Because the strategic and policy aspects of most countries were unprepared to deal with this serious epidemic crisis. India has not been spared from this epidemic this year. Yet it has partnered with itself in a concerted effort to combat the epidemic. In response to the disaster, the government enacted the Prevention of Epidemic Disease Act of 1897. The Disaster Management Act of 2005 took the advice of medical experts in a less decisive way for policymakers to make the epidemic a national emergency[1]. The epidemic has had a lasting effect on India's foreign policy. The second wave of Covid-19 and its tragic consequences have forced India to accept foreign aid after 17 years. It is bound to have far-reaching strategic implications for India. India's demand for regional supremacy and leadership could be a major blow as a direct result of the epidemic. These will affect the content and conduct of India's foreign policy in the years to come.

The impact of covid-19 on India's foreign policy has led to a decline in India's traditional dominance in the regional arena, material aid, and political influence. The Covid-19 has reduced its ability to help neighbours materially. Because historical ties alone cannot sustain India's regional hegemony. Thought check book diplomacy is already pushing India into its strategic location, the Indian subcontinent[2]. The second wave of the Covid-19 accelerated this process. Because India's ability to stand up to

China has greatly diminished today. Affects India's involvement with Covid-19. Any ambitious military spending will prevent modernization plans. It will limit the country's focus on global diplomacy and regional geopolitics. With reduced military spending and diplomatic focus on regional geopolitics, India's power will become uncertain.

2.0 Objectives of the Study:

1. The study wills emphasis the various importances of COVID-19 Vaccine.

2. To highlight various ways to create such an COVID-19 Vaccination among young and future generation in our society.

3. The study will suggest the COVID-19 Vaccination for future generation in our Nation.

4. The study will discuss about the various benefits and advantage of COVID-19 Vaccination.

5. The study will conduct how we can promote COVID-19 Vaccination awareness.

3.0 Who has influenced diplomacy in the Indo-Pacific Region:

The effects of Covid-19 have affected economies in the Indo-Pacific region. Unable to play a leading role in the Indo-Pacific project, China has tried to persuade smaller states in the region. And moving forward with the goal of exclusive dominance. Covid-19 is heading for a general economic crisis. As a result, the decline in foreign direct investment and industrial production and rising unemployment are expected to limit India's strategic ambitions. This suggests that Indian foreign policy in the aftermath of Covid-19 may therefore be a holding operation.

Indo-China relations:

Although India and China made a positive start in 2020, the epidemic began to rupture relations immediately. Significant tensions have spread on the border between the two countries. Troops and weapons were completely withdrawn from the north and south shores of Pangong Lake in February, through military and economic talks between India and China since early May 2020. Separate talks are now underway between the fear parties to deal with the remaining clashes. The Indian government banned Chinese products and Chinese apps, especially after the Galloway conflict. At present India-China relations are fragile and it is time to choose between protectionism and full cooperation. It is unknown at this time what he will do after leaving the post[3].

Indo-US relations:

The challenge of the covid epidemic and the change in the US administration have increased the dynamism of the ever-evolving relationship between the two strong democracies. It signed important defence agreements last year. Working towards a formal cut to the Quiet Alliance or actively supporting India during LAC urbanization with China. The Malabar exercise, which took place in November 2020, was a high point in the Indo-US strategic relationship, among the navies of the four quadruple countries. For the first time in three years, a mega naval exercise was held, which sent a strong message to China. However, there have been some ups and downs in Indo-US relations during the epidemic. While the United States was dealing with a deadly covid wave, India helped by providing medical supplies and exports and relaxing export restrictions. However, at the beginning of 2021, when India was going through the same ordeal, the United States was hesitant to show sincerity. The Joe Biden administration's U.S. First Policy the United States quickly changed course and accelerated supplies amid a storm of widespread condemnation around the world. Now is the time when epidemics are still rampant and vaccines are becoming increasingly necessary. Strong Indo-US relations will be important to help prevent global epidemics[4].

The partnership between the United States and India is bound up with a commitment to freedom, democratic principles, equality for all its citizens, and human rights. The United States and India share a common interest in promoting global security, resilience, and economic prosperity through trade investment and similar structures. But during the second wave of the Covid-19 epidemic, there was a delay in US approval of the raw materials needed to make the vaccine in India. At the behest of the public, however, Mohammad Adar Punawala, CO of the Seram Institute of India, played a key role in the outcry against this strong notion, which initially formed the backdrop of Indian foreign policy. However, the United States later revised its position on the issue, and the entire US leadership immediately began sending medical aid to India. They also contacted Indian leader Narendra Modi by phone. Internally, Jute has written realism and is expected to regain its brilliance in the last 4-5 years to show its inclination towards the United States[5]. Indian Foreign Minister Jayashankar, during his visit to New York and Washington, has so far focused on increasing vaccine production and distribution. He called for an agreement at the Security Dialogue Summit in March. Foreign Minister Biden emphasized the need for an intellectual property right over vaccines and other products, such as medical devices and personal protective equipment. The Foreign Minister met with corporate interrogators, including a new global task force, which has further helped raise funds for India.

India-Bangladesh relations:

On March 15, 2020, the Prime Minister of Bangladesh Sheikh Hasina took part in an online video conference with the leaders of SAARC countries at the invitation of Prime Minister Narendra Modi on the current state of the Kovid-19 epidemic. India and Bangladesh have excellent bilateral relations due to their common language, heritage, history, and culture. Since the agenda of the meeting was to stop the spread of the virus, a number of collaborative measures were discussed. 30000 tests including 30000 surgical masks, 15000 headcovers, 50000 surgical gloves, 100000 hydroxychloroquine medicine tablets, and RT-PCR test kits are discussed. In 2021, the Government of India has gifted 2 million covishild vaccines to Bangladesh to help it overcome the epidemic. The Government of Bangladesh has signed a bilateral MOU to procure 30 million doses of covid-19 vaccine from Bangladesh Beximco Pharmaceuticals Limited and the Serum Institute of India[6].

4.0 Medical diplomacy:

Historically, India has always been marked by poverty and disease. Even the colonists often painted a picture of an environment full of perpetual plague. Although India has certainly been known since those days. For many years the world has seen the nation not as a provider but as a recipient of global healthcare. However, India's role as an international healthcare provider in the epidemic has changed and its medical diplomacy has moved forward. From hydroxychloroquine medicine to vaccine delivery, India is reaching out to everyone in need. On January 21, 2021, India started promoting its vaccine alliance. Vasudeva Kutumbakam is a family venture inspired by the ancient Indian philosophical doctrine. Oxford AstraZeneca and the Serum Institute of India have provided Covi-shield vaccine, developed in neighbouring Bhutan and the Maldives, in a campaign under Rubric, India's first neighbour policy[7].

India has expanded its presence in South Asia by supplying vaccines to its neighbours Bangladesh, Bhutan, Nepal, Sri Lanka (excluding Pakistan and China) through vaccine alliance initiatives. However, the second wave of pandemic vaccines in India has temporarily suspended the alliance initiative. Trying to increase the impact of thinking about his opportunities. The second wave of the Covid-19 epidemic forced K to accept foreign aid, including the Chinese Red Cross, for the first time in 16 years. The Bhartiya Janata Party-led government of India has to seek foreign aid, which is a shame. This is because seeking help from outside or relying on outsiders is a thundering signal in Indian foreign policy. The call for a virtual conference of South Asian foreign ministers on China's recent vaccine[8] cooperation will have a long-term effect. To free China from its influence in South Asia in the short term, India must first work to earn its credibility internally. For more than two decades, India has earned the reputation of being the "Pharmacy of the World". Because of its strong generic pharmaceutical industry, it has been providing quality medicines at affordable prices in the world market. India has taken steps to reduce the cost of treating affordable AIDS, tuberculosis, and malaria at a time when the Indian company HIV is spreading worldwide. India's generic industry has emerged as the largest supplier. Moreover, the export of medicines from India has indeed increased from 1 1 billion at the beginning of the century to now 20 billion. It plays a historic role as a supplier of affordable medicines. India has taken two significant initiatives to overcome the Covid-19 epidemic. The first is to make vaccines widely available, making the Covid-19 vaccine universally acceptable. Second, the initiative is to submit a joint proposal with South Africa to the WTO, which would provide a temporary exemption from the exercise and exercise of intellectual property rights. The purpose is to try to free the Covid-19 vaccine, medicine, and other medical products from intellectual property rights[9].

On 19 April 2021, the Press Information Bureau released details of India's Covid-19 vaccination strategy, focusing on the scale and speed of the third phase. The National Expert Group on Vaccine Administration for Covid-19, chaired by Dr. V K Pal, a member of the Policy Commission, played a key role in developing the strategy. The first phase of India's Covid-19 mass inflation program was launched on January 16. An estimated 30 million healthcare and frontline workers were covered. On March 1, Vision launched the second phase, which aimed to cover the illnesses of people over 45 and those over 60. The deadline for vaccinating all people over the age of 45 has been extended to April 1. As a result, over 300 million vaccines have been given. Although only 22 percent of the population[10].

In March 2021, India emerged as one of the leading suppliers of the Covid-19 vaccine. Rainfall has been able to play this role due to its partnership with the Serum Institute of India, the world's largest vaccine manufacturer in terms of dosage. The company claims that it is capable of producing 1.5 billion doses annually. In June 2020, SII signed an agreement with AstraZeneca. It is a British Swedish pharmaceutical company. Oxford University will supply 1 billion doses of the covid vaccine to middle and low-income countries, including India. SII is currently supplying its vaccine "Covi shield" to the Government of India.

5.0 How many companies are providing vaccines in India? :

Vaccination is an important part of India's fight against the second Covid-19 wave. Vaccinating about 150 million (850 million) people over the age of 18 is a major challenge for the country. This means that India currently needs 17.7 million vaccines for the entire vaccine. The government has said that India will produce a total of 126 crore vaccines between August and December. The target is to collect more than 35.6 crore doses. However, due to the current inability of India to meet the demand for biotics, the Serum Institute, the world's largest vaccine maker, and Russia's Sputnik 'V Kovid Nineteen Vaccine' have been contracted to arrive in India on 31 May 2021 with the first large consignment of millions. Russia has provided 2 million doses[11].

What is Co-vaxine?:

Covaxine is an inactivated vaccine, meaning it is made up of a dead coronavirus. This makes the body safe for injection. Biotic India is a 24-year-old vaccine maker with a portfolio of 16 vaccines and exports to 123 countries. The coronavirus tips isolated by the National Institute of Virology of India used a sample. When administered the immune cells can recognize the still dead virus. The epidemic causes the immune system to produce antibodies against the virus. Two doses are given four weeks apart. The vaccine can be stored at temperatures ranging from 2-degree Celsius to 8 degreeCelsius. The effectiveness of the vaccine is 81%. Shows preliminary data from its phase trial. India's regulator gave emergency approval to the vaccine in January. When the third phase of the trial was underway. Experts say India Biotech says it has 20 million doses of vaccine in stock. It aims to produce 700 million doses of its four facilities in the two cities by the end of the year.

What is covishild?:

The Oxford AstraZeneca vaccine is being manufactured locally at the Seram Institute of India, the world's largest vaccine manufacturer. It says it made more than 60 million per month. When it is injected into a patient, it triggers the immune system to produce antibodies. Helps to attack any coronavirus infection. The vaccine is given in two doses four to 12 weeks apart. It can be safely stored at temperatures from 2 degrees Celsius to 1 degree Celsius. Doctors can be easily delivered to existing healthcare settings like surgery. The vaccine was developed by Pfizer- Biotech which is currently being operated in several countries. Must be stored at 70 0 C. Only a limited number of jars can be removed. A special challenge in India because summer temperatures there can reach up to 50 degrees Celsius.

What is Sputnik V?:

The vaccine, developed by the Moscow Camellia Institute, initially sparked some controversy after it rolled out before final test data were released. But scientists say the benefits have now been demonstrated. It uses a cold virus designed to infect the body as a carrier to deliver a small piece of coronavirus. Thus, a part of the genetic defect of the virus can safely expose the body and fight against it without the risk of getting sick. After vaccination, the body begins to produce antibodies to the coronavirus. It can be stored at temperatures up to 8 degrees Celsius from Today Grit which is easy to transport and store.

India's Sputnik V:

According to the report, the Russian direct investment fund, TT Vaccine Marketing, has entered into agreements with six domestic vaccine manufacturers to manufacture 750 million doses of Sputnik V in India. Dr. Reddy's Laboratories, head of pharmaceuticals in Hyderabad, will import the first batch of 125 million doses to India this quarter. The level will be increased in the next quarter when the Indian company starts building under the supervision of Dr. Reddy. Until the day, India will largely rely on the two previously approved candidates, Covacin and Covishield[12].

6.0 Government of India and Vaccine Diplomacy:

The Government of India has announced a comprehensive vaccine diplomacy strategy to provide a significant number of vaccines to most of its neighbours and other developing countries, including Africa. India has seven neighbouring countries in South Asia such as Afghanistan, Bangladesh, Bhutan, Maldives, Nepal, and Sri Lanka. All countries that have already received vaccine assistance are Myanmar and Mauritius. In a South Asian region where China's growing presence has been evident over the years, the Indian government's vaccine diplomacy could play a key role. The real value of India's vaccine diplomacy can be seen in the fact that Canadian Prime Minister Trudeau sought Prime Minister Modi's help in getting the vaccine from SII. But relations between India and Canada have been bitter for months. So, India's vaccine diplomacy has helped normalize.

The Government of India's policy of vaccination with partner countries will undoubtedly serve the welfare of the people of the world. Vaccines and affordable medicine are at the heart of the prospect of a rapid recovery of the global economy from the Cavs 90 crisis. To this end, especially for the citizens of developing countries, India and South Africa took an important initiative to ensure the affordable price of Covid-19 vaccine-related products through their proposal to the WTO in October 2020[13].

Country	Commercial	Supply	Total
Bangladesh	2000	7000	9000
Marocco	0	7000	7000
Brazil	0	4000	4000
Myanmar	1700	2000	3700
SaudiArabia	0	3000	3000
Nepal	1000	1000	2000
SriLankan	500	500	1000
South Africa	0	1000	1000
Mexico	0	870	870
Ghana	0	600	600
Argentina	0	580	580
Afghanistan	500	0	500
Ukraine	0	500	500
Maldives	200	0	200
Mauritius	100	100	200
Kuwait	0	200	200
United Arab Emirates	0	200	200
Bhutan	150	0	150
Srebia	0	150	150
Magnolia	150	0	150
Bahrain	100	0	100
Oman	100	0	100
Bark dose	100	0	100
UNO	0	100	100
Dominica	70	0	70
Seychelles	50	0	50
Egypt	0	50	50
Algeria	0	50	50
Democratic Republic	30	20	50
L Salvador	0	20	20
Total	6750	28940	35690

Source: foreign ministry of India

8.0 Challenges of Vaccination and Homeschooling for Parents:

Since the closure of k-12 schools, parents find themselves primarily responsible for the teaching of their children and they are forced to take over the task of vaccination and home-schooling to maintain continuity of education, understanding, learning, etc. as it is an added burden, while they are already tackling issues such as work-from-home, temporary unemployment leading to financial crisis, management of household problems, etc.and many parents would not have adequate time or the necessary educational qualifications to assist their children with classwork, assignments that were previously taken care of by their teachers, which is likely to lead to frustration and burnout amongst caregivers and disruption in the academic activities of the children, leading to stress in both parents and children in general. Gender disparity regarding vaccination, allocation of household duties in such periods of confinement also needs to be focused upon, as women are often expected to devote more time to home-schooling children and doing household chores affecting their academic career (Machado et al., 2019). Both teachers and students are unprepared in terms of technology handling/accessibility issues for online learning where most of the academic activities happen byzoom, google meet etc. online learning platform (Jena, 2020).

9.0 Conclusion:

In this complex and uncertain time, India's diplomacy has borne fruit in adapting and evolving. All wealth is achieved by growth periods. An economic upsurge occurred after World War II and the Great Depression, and a similar trend was observed after the death of the four greats in the aftermath of World War II. The health crisis has led to significant investments in medicine and public health. The same is expected after the epidemic and India must rise from its responsibility. It is imperative that Kovid-19 goes beyond diplomacy, geopolitics and works for the real welfare of the people in the spirit of Basudev Kutumbakam. In the years to come, India should have a proactive and dynamic global strategy.

References:

- Smriti kurup, " impact of covid-19 on India's foreign policy: an analysis", August 6, 2021
- Biswajit Dhar, "India's vaccine diplomacy" April 8, 2021
- Smriti kurup, " impact of covid-19 on India's foreign policy: an analysis", August 6, 2021

- Smriti kurup, " impact of covid-19 on India's foreign policy: an analysis", August 6, 2021
- Rachit Garg, "Indian foreign policy during the covid-19 pandemic" August 2021

- Rachit Garg, "Indian foreign policy during the covid-19 pandemic" August 2021

- Anuttama Banarjee, " India's flawed vaccine diplomacy", June 25, 2021
- Jabint Jacob,"indias waxing diplomacy failure and its foreign policy implications", May 19, 2021
- Biswajit Dhar, "India's vaccine diplomacy" April 8, 2021
- Covid-19 vaccines in India, BBC, May 31,2021

- Covid-19 vaccines in India, BBC, May 31,2021

CHAPTER TEN

School Students Academic Stress And Anxiety In The Covid-19 Vaccination

-----**Dr. Kotra Balayogi*

Introduction

Stress and anxiety have a negative effect on the quality of Indian k-12 students' life, their education and career, also may cause drop out from the schools, during an epidemic/pandemic state, during the vaccination proves k-12 students are exposed to additional anxiety and stressful factors, such as fear of being infected and coping with anxiety and stress is extremely important on health. The latest research studying coping strategies of students and k-12 learning and teaching during the covid-19 pandemic in India and k-12 students used problem-focused coping and strategies in get rid from stress and anxiety even after the vaccination, and in Israel during the covid-19 pandemic, a state-wide mandatory closure of all k-12 schools from the beginning of March 2020 and an isolation policy was introduced by the government. The staff of all academic k-12 institutions faced a new reality had to turn to online teaching with the aim of continuing the academic year and trying to carry out end-of-semester exams as usual and all staff members started to practice and use remote teaching strategies almost immediately with the lockdown. The objective of this study was to assess after the vaccination, the level of anxiety, stress, and ways of coping during the period of covid-19 pandemic and identify the association of coping strategies with characteristics of the k-12 students in India, to assess the prevalence and severity of core symptoms of depression, anxiety and stress in k-12 students across India during the lock-down and to estimate the impact of lock-down on time spent on their routine activities, domestic violence, eating habits and sleep pattern; to analyze the impact of various factors and the mental health status after the process of vaccination.

Challenges Of Vaccination And Home Schooling For Parents

Since the closure of k-12 schools, parents find themselves primarily responsible for the teaching of their children and they are forced to take over the task of vaccination and home-schooling to maintain continuity of education, understanding, learning, etc. as it is an added burden, while they are already tackling issues such as work-from-home, temporary unemployment leading to the financial crisis, management of household problems, etc. and many parents would not have adequate time or the necessary educational qualifications to assist their children with classwork, assignments that were previously taken care of by their teachers, which is likely to lead to frustration and burnout amongst caregivers and disruption in the academic activities of the children, leading to stress in both parents and children in general. Gender disparity regarding vaccination, allocation of household duties in such periods of confinement also needs to be focused upon, as women are often expected to devote more time to home-schooling children and doing household chores affecting their academic career (Machado et al., 2019). Both teachers and students are unprepared in terms of technology handling/accessibility issues for online learning where most of the academic activities happen by zoom, google meet, etc. online learning platforms (Jena, 2020).

Digital Learning Towards K-12 Schooling

While the majority of k-12 schools are transitioned to online delivery of classes and evaluation to avoid the disruption of educational services, the digital platform still remains uncharted territory for the majority of people in a low-middle income country like India. The internet penetration in India is making steady inroads into urban as well as rural areas, and approximately 73.3% of the country's population is said to be connected by mobile phones (Sood et al., 2019), but the utilization of digital resources especially in mainstream education had remained virtually unexplored as of now. Secondly, dissemination of learning through a digital portal would require access to a laptop/computer for the students, which given the disparity amongst the socio-economic strata, remains unattainable for students belonging to low-income groups. According to National Sample Survey, 2017-18, 24% of households have an internet facility and only 8% of all households with members aged between five and 24 have both a computer and an internet connection (Ministry of Statistics and Program

Implementation, 2017–2018). This disparity of access becomes a harbinger of academic stress in students who would find themselves unable to avail themselves of online classes or submit their assignments, thus falling behind their peers in their curriculum. This has led to reports of symptoms of depression, anxiety, poverty, and in severe cases suicidal attempts in k-12 children and adolescents triggered by academic stress and apprehensions regarding the future (Fegert et al., 2020). The absence of adequate social welfare and policy measures at governmental and institutional levels leads to a severe mental health crisis amongst the young, further weakening their academic prospects leading to a vicious cycle of mental disorders, academic underachievement, and poor socio-occupational functioning in India.

The Psychological Effect Of Academic Stress And Anxiety

Students in a secondary education setting are known to face a varied range of ongoing normative stressors and anxiety associated with their ongoing academic demands however, in the current scenario created by the social restrictions imposed by the pandemic, have led to escalation to severe levels of academic stress and anxiety in k-12 students. There is enough evidence to demonstrate that severe and long-standing academic-related stress has an adverse effect on academic performance, mental health and well-being of children and adolescents. Academic-related stress and anxiety is significantly associated with reduced student academic motivation (Liu, 2015) and academic disengagement (Liu & Lu, 2011). This in turn makes them vulnerable to dropping out, future unemployment, and increased incidence of psychiatric disorders such as depression, anxiety and substance use disorders (Pascoe et al., 2020). Long-standing stress and anxiety exposure in k-12 children and adolescents may also lead to the development of physical health problems such as metabolic syndrome, obesity and reduced insulin sensitivity as well as reduction of life expectancy (Pervanidou & Chrousos, 2012).

Need For Policy Measures

The COVID-19 pandemic has grown from being a public health crisis to an overarching humanitarian crisis demanding strong social welfare measures to mitigate its adverse consequences and the k-12 education sector in India is one important area that has been severely affected by the lockdown and restrictions that are required to slow down the disease transmission (Sharma, 2020). Although the department of school literacy and education is involved in improving access to education through various online platforms and initiatives like National Repository of Open

Educational Resources (NROER), Digital Infrastructure for Knowledge Sharing (DIKSHA), e-Pathshala and a National Online Education platform called SWAYAM (Ministry of Statistics and Program Implementation, 2017–2018), etc. but the accessibility and acceptability of such initiatives need to be focused upon as much as possible (Jena, 2020).

Healthy Ways To Manage Stress And Anxiety

- Confront the Stressor
- Proper Time Management
- Being Organized
- Exercise, Nutrition, and Sleep
- Spending Time with the Loved Ones
- Taking a Break

Conclusion And Discussion

Epidemics and pandemics are not new to humans, such diseases besides bringing loss to human lives also bring many adverse impacts on individuals and society especially for k-12 students. COVID-19 being one such pandemic has terrifically affected the lives of people and as a measure to contain it, governments are imposing lock-downs. Hence the present study aimed at assessing the stress and anxiety, psychological impact of the lock-down towards k-12 children across India. In less than a few months, the COVID-19 pandemic has created an emergency state globally and this contagious virus has not only raised concerns over general public health but has also caused a number of psychological and mental disorders and the COVID-19 pandemic can affect stress, anxiety and mental health in k-12 students and different communities. Therefore, in the current crisis, it is vital to identify high school students prone to psychological disorders from different groups and at different layers of populations, so that with appropriate psychological strategies, techniques and interventions, the general population's mental health is preserved and improved. COVID-19 not only causes physical health concerns but also results in a number of psychological disorders and the spread of the new coronavirus can impact the mental health of people in different communities. Thus, it is essential to preserve the mental health of individuals and to develop psychological interventions that can improve the mental health of vulnerable groups during the COVID-19 pandemic. Despite the limitations of the present study related to a cross-sectional design with self-reported measures, these findings add new evidence concerning anxiety and stress among k-12 students during the pandemic of covid-19 and the teachers of the belief that the most important way to help students during this period is to stay in continuous contact with parents beyond online teaching and learning. Students face severe stress and anxiety related to economic uncertainty, fear for the health of their families, fear of infection, the need to support and care for children, and dealing with the challenges of online distance education.

Teaching techniques and college environments should be adapted to the needs of the students. The productive utilization of existing student welfare systems, development of more 'student-friendly' environments, and regular periodic extracurricular activities with universal participation can prove to be useful stress-busters. Similarly, students living in hostels were observed to be prone to develop stress; thus, a periodic review of hostels, with feedback from the students, should be conducted and the complaints of students should be promptly addressed. The majority of students were in favor of stress management education being included in the curriculum, and hence steps should be taken for its incorporation. Health is a major concern of students, and therefore the promotion of healthy dietary and lifestyle habits should be encouraged. Additionally, teachers, parents, and even students themselves should be aware that undue expectations about academic achievement can lead to stress.

Finally, regular study habits and adequate preparation can help students to avoid stress and make their learning effective. The main goal of the school education department faculty in the country is to keep in touch with students, to encourage and support them through this challenging period, which is still far from being finished as these words are being written. Additional research is being planned in the near future to assess whether there has been a change in the state of stress and anxiety of the k-12 students and their use of various coping strategies to meet the challenges of the situation and future studies needed to suggest and to assess the methods for reducing stress and anxiety among k-12 students in India.

Recommendations

The corona outbreak created a world of ambiguity, loss of control, and uncertainty and the feeling of losing control is very stressful for the general population and especially for k-12 students and the faculty has an important role to create a sense of control and provide a stable educational structure for the students. Maintaining a stable educational framework, including reducing to a minimum any changes in the teaching schedule, announcing information about changes as soon as possible, supplying updated information about the continuance of the academic year and exams. The policy of maximum schedule stabilization during the lockdown was successfully introduced in k-12 education in addition, students who were parents of children got special consideration as at the same hours of their classes, their k-12 children also needed to participate in distance learning, making it challenging, as not every family has more than one computer. These students were not obligated for synchronous participation in lectures and classes, and all lessons teaching were recorded and supplied for them and online teaching workshops were delivered to ensure high-quality teaching. Additional effort should be made to prepare k-12 students for epidemic related challenges and build professional competency in secondary teachers of regular and special schools in delivering online teaching, special focus on students from marginalized sections and CWD, improve penetration of electronic media and internet connectivity across geographical locations and various socio-economic strata and upscaling of technological infrastructure at all areas in the country.

References

- American Psychological Association (APA), (2020, May 30). Stress in the time of COVID 19. Retrieved on 07/07/2020.
- Choudhary, R. (2020, April 16). COVID-19 Pandemic: Impact and strategies for the education sector in India. https://government.economictimes.indiatimes.com/news/education/covid-19-pandemic-impact-and-strategies-for-education-sector-in-india/75173099
- Dangi RR, George M. Psychological Perception of Students During COVID-19 Outbreak in India Psychological Perception of Students During COVID-19 Outbreak in India. High Technol Lett [Internet]. 2020;26(6):142–78. Available from:
- https://www.researchgate.net/publication/342094992_Psychological_Perception_of_Students_During_COVID-19_Outbreak_in_India
- Goyal, K., Chauhan, P., Chhikara, K., Gupta, P., & Singh, M. (2020). Fear of COVID 2019: First suicidal case in India! Asian Journal of Psychiatry, 49,
- 101989. https://doi.org/10.1016/j.ajp.2020.101989.

- Jena, P. (2020). Impact of pandemic COVID-19 on education in India. International Journal of Current Research, 12, 12582–12586.
- Kumar, A., & Nayar, K. R. (2020). COVID 19 and its mental health consequences. Journal of Mental Health. https://doi.org/10.1080/09638237.2020.1757052.
- Roy, D., Tripathy, S., Kar, S., Sharma, N., Verma, S., & Kaushal, V. (2020). Study of knowledge, attitude, anxiety & perceived mental healthcare need in Indian population during COVID-19 pandemic. Asian Journal of Psychiatry, 51, 102083. https://doi.org/10.1016/j.ajp.2020.102083.
- Saha S, Dutta T, A Study on the Psychological Crisis during the Lock-down caused due to Covid-19 Pandemic. Afric J Biol Medic Resea. 2020;3(2):41-9.
- Sahu, P. (2020). Closure of universities due to Coronavirus Disease 2019 (COVID-19): Impact on education and mental health of students and academic staff. Cureus, 12(4).
- Sood S. Psychological effects of the Coronavirus disease-2019 pandemic. Resea Humanit Medic Educat. 2020; 7:23-6.
- Sinha, A. (2014). Stress vs Academic Performance. SCMS Journal of Indian Management, 11(4), p. 46.
- World Health Organization. Mental Health and Psychosocial Considerations During COVID-19 Outbreak [Internet]. World Health Organization. 2020. Available from: https://www.who.int/docs/defaultsource/coronaviruse/mental-healthconsiderations.pdf?sfvrsn=6d3578af_2. WHO. Coronavirus Disease (COVID-19) Dashboard. Retrieved on June 3, 2020. From https://covid19.who.int/

CHAPTER ELEVEN

Post-Covid Challenges And Coping Strategies For Retail Industry In India: An Empirical Study

------*Dr.V.P.Sriram**Prof. (Dr) Aruna Anchal*

Introduction

As we all know that from 2019 onwards still now the whole world is facing a pandemic period called covid-19. Which caused many deaths, mental anxiety, physical disorders, fights, riots, and many more. The older citizen is very prone to this disease, but at the same time children and teenagers are also facing many problems of not getting independent socially. It is a very crucial time for the world population to maintain the situation by following some rules and regulations adapted by the government and personally too (Ajmal, et. al,2021).

Average Shoppers spend more money in physical stores than they do on online because businesses in physical form are more likely to spur spontaneous purchases, especially at a time when people are cutting back on their outings. Customers are exposed to a wide range of items in stores, which might be difficult to sift through in an online catalogue. The use of internet has increased these days so it is helpful for many people to get aware of the updates of covid-19. Not only getting aware of the situation the social media is playing a very vital role these days because by this way people are getting ways to attach to their close ones, friends, relatives. This social media has also played a role for educational purpose as the schools, colleges, high schools and universities are closed down due to this pandemic situation. Generally, teenagers engage themselves in social media to keeps themselves attached to their close friends and so on. But on the other hand, in many families the child abuse cases has also given rise, for which the children and teenagers especially are committing suicide. The suicide cases have also risen. Covid-19 is a shock to society, health, economics and the governments worldwide. The pressure on the population as well as the coordinators and governments itself to tackle with this pandemic situation is an extraordinary challenge to mage the impact of this situation and its consequences (Schleper, et. al, 2021)

Many motivational speakers said that after the covid-19 there is a big risk that the world could be divided and nationalistic. Here politics could turn toxic if the government is unable to recover the people from the pandemic as soon as possible. As the pandemic started the trade business in the world-wide area i.e., domestic and international trades are going down eventually day by day. The closing of borders and not coordinating the rules internationally will make it even more difficult to start the trade, travel purposes, higher anxiety and anger and lastly lockdown (Sharma, et. al, 2021). Figure 1 presents the major post Covid Challenges for Retail Industry:

Figure 1 Post Covid Challenges for Retail Industry, Source: Authors

As the novel coronavirus spreads all over the world the states individually is enforcing to do social distancing by outgoing to places such as restaurants, bars and retailers to face the problematic situation. Covid-19 has dramatically disrupted the retail sector with the pandemic shock. "India is the world's fifth-largest global destination in retail space whereas in FDI India is ranked 16th after US, Canada, Germany, UK, China, Japan, France, Australia, Switzerland and Italy" (Alonso, et. al, 2020).

Literature Review

The covid-19 crisis has affected the societies, economics, all over the world. After the covid situation the world is provided with a range of experts who is giving opinion and also will help in future for a sustainable life by some of these, the planning for the world after covid-19, opportunities for regional organizations, cities in the time of the pandemic, sustain globalization, technology and digital future life, trade and connectivity, the pandemic that stopped the world, providing health for free, a socio-psychological perspective. The coronavirus disease is distressing life worldwide (Chowdhury, et. al, 2020). From now to beyond, consumer behaviour (how people consume, shop, live, utilise technology, work, and move) will evolve across three horizons. Consumers are storing critical commodities, and e-commerce and digital payments are on the rise, while *Kirana* stores continue to draw smaller audiences in both urban and rural locations. A daily living will resume in the following phase, although consumer confidence will be harmed due to health and economic worries. Consumers will trade down and consume cheaper/private label brands, reducing brand loyalty. The importance of focusing on one's health will grow. New online shoppers, such as the elderly and those living in remote areas, will continue to use the internet. Rural customers, on the other hand, will continue to survive on necessities. Beyond the crisis, online adoption will continue to rise.

The practice of segregation, contact limitations, folds up of the shops, schools, and colleges caused a complete change in the mental and psychological surroundings in pretty every single country. These closures had a great significant threat to the lives of children and teenagers especially. During this situation there are many advantages and disadvantages included, but the level of disadvantages are more than advantages such as be deficient in of contact, abridged opportunities, pressure regulations, parental psychological sickness, household aggression and children mistreatment, disturbance experience, low socioeconomic status, poverty, and disabilities are the main challenges faced after or as we say post covid situations. Recovered patients have faced weakness, memory loss, anxiety, depression and many other issues. It seems very difficult to get recovered after covid because even a person who hardly had any symptoms and was positive experienced syndrome-like fatigue, severe headache, body ache, which made the people more uncomfortable these days. These symptoms can be in a body for at least 6 months, so it is very important to be careful and attentive to the updates of this virus. The dealings with this symptom include taking proper rest, having a good diet, little exercise, regular health check-ups, keep self- updated (Hossain, 2018). The post-Covid situation also includes economic and social disturbances like poverty, unemployment, less food availability, loss of livelihood. This pandemic has given problems rouse to the entire food system, border closure, trade including buying and selling products and do marketing. Millions of farmers, workers face malnutrition, health facilities due to financial problems as well as other abuses. Conversely, some industries have seen noteworthy growth together with skill service, residence amusement, hospitals, medicinal suppliers, e-commerce retailers, delivery services, courier services, and computer-generated security. Now, the pandemic situation has everything towards online platforms so the means of getting engaged to the digital world is cheaper and great to access with better productivity and providing many opportunities. This made communication between people worldwide very much easier (Butt, 2021). A merchant may pick from a variety of data suppliers in the age of big data. Understanding existing client demands and potential future customers requires accurate data. GIS technology can relate demographics like as age, gender, income, and purchasing patterns to a physical place or catchment area, allowing companies to discover opportunities and specify actions.

Coming to the educational sectors post covid pandemic, it has created a big threat to the students all over the world. Analytics with the help of data might appear cold and too much clinical at times, but when it delivers actionable knowledge, it can help merchants build stronger relationships with their consumers. In this unique retail era, location information enables companies to meet customers on their terms in a variety of ways, large and small. Nearly “1.6 billion students is out of school in 161 countries which is the 80% of world’s enrolled students”. The world is facing an educational crisis too. The students are facing losses in learning, dropouts because of low family finances, and many children who lives on midday meals. Richer countries can afford to get into the digital world of education but there are many countries that are unable to provide these facilities to their students (Deshmukh, & Haleem, 2020). The teachers and parents are facing problems to educate their children during this pandemic situation. The pandemic also raises scientific challenges that necessitate being answered. The importance of science, the enlargement of industry, and the function of the state in a pandemic have recently received little consideration from society. Many opportunities to be considered throughout the donor community go beyond "single" product-based interventions to consider processes and paradigms. Strive to balance the Innovation for Development portfolio with a focus on forward-looking predictive innovation and bottom-up adaptive innovation. Investing in more strategic and focused collaborations, especially with local and national stakeholders to make sure and maintain that the poorest people are the focus and no one is left behind (Chowdhury, et. al, 2020).

In winding up, the innovation for development agenda's performance was promising, yet inconsistent. Many projects and programmes have outperformed expectations and provided really revolutionary and large-scale development impacts. These include lowering the cost and increasing access to vaccines and medicines in the poorest countries, promoting financial inclusion and SME development through mobile money and microfinance, and tackling malnutrition and hygiene through a community-based approach that includes the use of cash transfers to improve food security. Improve catastrophe and climate change resilience by using insurance and other adaptation strategies (Sharma, et. al, 2020).

Mechanism for Retailers

The pandemic brings with itself an uncounted number of uncertainties in the surrounding which makes it a crisis; merchants must have a cross-functional rapid reaction team in place to address any subsequent events. They must be adaptive and flexible enough to change operating models and product offerings to address the most pressing need at any given time. First of all the retailers converted the huge bulk of buyers to online services, they are approaching to the apps online to maintain the sales in the business these days, while shopping online the product of your need will be obviously transported by a delivery guy so one can bring change in the pattern of delivery to maintain the social distancing, moving the general gate meetings performed in the streets are avoided and are given platforms such as Google meet, zoom, WhatsApp etc (Sharma, et. al, 2020). In these difficult economic times, one of the most crucial things a business can take is to ensure that the proper products and in-demand items are in stock. Bestsellers should be prominently displayed, and popular secondary goods such as accessories should be easily accessible. It's a crucial retail strategy that will outlive the pandemic—and one that varies greatly depending on store location. Analyzing establishments with high click-and-collect rates can help retailers discover new ways to engage with customers. Merchandise planners can figure out what items are frequently transported to certain places and find a similar item in the shop. When the consumer picks up their order, the on-site staff can display them the complementary product based on that information. Some forward-thinking retailers are responding to the realities of COVID-19 by physically placing their products where their consumers are—with pop-up stores and even trucks. It's a tendency that's likely to persist until the epidemic is over, and a small number of retailers are already mastering it. Denim firms in India, such as Pepe Jeans and Levi Strauss & Co., have responded to sluggish traffic in traditional shopping malls by sending retail trucks to residential areas. These mobile stores are stocked with trendy work-at-home outfits and can take customer measurements and arrange for products to be sent following alterations. It's the type of dexterity and knowledge of one's surroundings that the situation necessitates. In order to do that due to coronavirus infection rates and business restrictions differing greatly by state and nation, the location of a store now has greater importance on its performance and potentially solvency. In order to cope, nimble merchants are examining catchment regions. After examinations, they try to open up small temporary outlets to sell their product to the potential customers. Retailers will have to repurpose their supply chains to accommodate demand changes within certain categories while dealing with supply restrictions. Until a business returns to normal, they must have the capacity to organize inventory and logistics across locations in a very dynamic manner. As the industry shifts to more multichannel and delivery-based models, digitization will aid in redesigning corporate processes and satisfying customer demand for speedy fulfillment. In the aftermath in order to retain customers, retailers must maintain contact with customers during the crisis. They must instill confidence in customers that appropriate measures will be taken to protect their health and safety. The situation has so far resulted in increased regulatory scrutiny and the issuance of several directives by municipal, state, and federal governments in order to safeguard safety and health. While following all of the directions can be time demanding (in terms of resources), it will be critical for retailers to work with regulatory agencies throughout the process as the lockdown is removed in phases.

Conclusion

Nobody can say with confidence what the material impact of the COVID-19 outbreak on the sector will be since it is still unfolding. This pandemic, however, should serve as a warning to immediately develop a flexible and adaptable business and operational strategy to deal with future disturbances. This will necessitate a strong focus on transforming into a digital business. Now is the moment for retailers to take control of the present crisis and invest in the development of a more robust business. In all OECD nations, the retail sector is the most significant. It is a gateway to consumers from the upstream industry, accounting for a significant amount of GDP and employing one out of every twelve people. COVID19 has thrown this industry into disarray, separating physical and online stores, required and non-mandatory stores, and small and large merchants. Coronavirus sickness continues to spread in an unexpected manner over the world. The speed and strength of recovery are determined by national health, humanitarian, and socioeconomic policies. Countries that now lack the financial capacity to implement social programs, particularly universal social security systems, require collaborative global initiatives. The long-term viability of debt should be a top focus. The deep-seated inequality highlighted by the crisis would be substantially greater if long-term structural adjustments were not made. In addition to dealing with the crisis's immediate implications, the world community now has a once-in-a-lifetime chance to take steps toward a future of social justice and people-centered activity (Vanapalli, et. al, 2021).

References

- Vanapalli, K. R., Sharma, H. B., Ranjan, V. P., Samal, B., Bhattacharya, J., Dubey, B. K., & Goel, S. (2021). Challenges and strategies for effective plastic waste management during and post COVID-19 pandemic. *Science of The Total Environment*, *750*, 141514.
- Sharma, A., Adhikary, A., & Borah, S. B. (2020). Covid-19′ s impact on supply chain decisions: Strategic insights from NASDAQ 100 firms using Twitter data. *Journal of Business Research*, *117*, 443-449.
- Sharma, G. D., Talan, G., & Jain, M. (2020). Policy response to the economic challenge from COVID-19 in India: A qualitative enquiry. *Journal of Public Affairs*, *20*(4), e2206.
- Chowdhury, M. T., Sarkar, A., Paul, S. K., & Moktadir, M. A. (2020). A case study on strategies to deal with the impacts of COVID-19 pandemic in the food and beverage industry. *Operations Management Research*, 1-13.
- Butt, A. S. (2021). Supply chains and COVID-19: impacts, countermeasures and post-COVID-19 era. *The International Journal of Logistics Management*.
- Alonso, A. D., Kok, S. K., Bressan, A., O'Shea, M., Sakellarios, N., Koresis, A., ... & Santoni, L. J. (2020). COVID-19, aftermath, impacts, and hospitality firms: An international perspective. *International journal of hospitality management*, *91*, 102654.
- Sharma, M., Luthra, S., Joshi, S., & Kumar, A. (2021). Accelerating retail supply chain performance against pandemic disruption: adopting

resilient strategies to mitigate the long-term effects. *Journal of Enterprise Information Management.*

- Schleper, M. C., Gold, S., Trautrims, A., & Baldock, D. (2021). Pandemic-induced knowledge gaps in operations and supply chain management: COVID-19's impacts on retailing. *International Journal of Operations & Production Management.*
- Ajmal, M. M., Khan, M., Shad, M. K., AlKatheeri, H., & Jabeen, F. (2021). The socio-economic and technological new normal in supply chain management: lessons from COVID-19 pandemic. *The International Journal of Logistics Management.*
- Hossain, S. T. (2018). Impacts of COVID-19 on the agri-food sector: Food security policies of Asian productivity organization members.
- Chowdhury, M. T., Sarkar, A., Paul, S. K., & Moktadir, M. A. (2020). A case study on strategies to deal with the impacts of the COVID-19 pandemic in the food and beverage industry. *Operations Management Research*, 1-13.
- Deshmukh, S. G., & Haleem, A. (2020). Framework for manufacturing in post-Covid-19 world order: an indian perspective. *International Journal of Global Business and Competitiveness, 15*, 49-60.

CHAPTER TWELVE

Innovation In Response To The Covid-19 Crisis

-----*Dr. Savita Mishra**Kanishka***Dr. Anshika Rajvanshi

Introduction

Many addiction treatment and harm reduction groups had to restrict their hours and services for persons with drug use problems during the COVID-19 epidemic, putting these people at danger of mortality. To address limited treatment access during COVID-19, the Substance Abuse Mental Health Services Administration, the US Drug Enforcement Administration, and the US Department of Health and Human Services issued guidance allowing for buprenorphine induction via audio-only telehealth encounters without requiring an in-person evaluation or video interface. This has allowed for new ideas to be developed in order to satisfy the requirements of the most vulnerable people throughout the present pandemic.

The COVID-19 pandemic has disrupted all aspects of academic medical center missions. The number and rapidity of innovative responses to the crisis are extraordinary. When the pandemic has subsided, the world of academic medicine will have changed.The author of this Invited Commentary anticipates that at least some of these innovations will become part of academic medicine's everyday clinical and educational operations. Here, he considers the implications of exemplary innovations—virtual care, hospital at home, advances in diagnosis and therapy, virtual learning, and virtual clinical learning—for regulators, academic medical centers, faculty, and students.

'Today the greatest risk of global catastrophe [is a virus]. If anything kills over ten million people in the next few decades, it's most likely to be a highly infectious virus rather than a war. Not missiles, but microbes. ... We are not ready for the next epidemic.'

—Bill Gates, TED talk, 2015

Source: dnaindia.com

The COVID-19 pandemic's demands on clinical care systems, interruptions in educational institutions, economic disarray, and societal upheaval are unparalleled in our collective memory. It may be exaggerating to call this an existential crisis for academic medical centres (AMCs), but it has ushered in a watershed moment. In addition, the speed and breadth of creative solutions generated in response to the crisis and applied throughout AMCs and their missions is unparalleled. The world will have altered after the epidemic has passed. What will the impact of the COVID-19 pandemic in 2020 be on medical educators and AMCs in the United States?

Innovation entails not only the production of new products, but also their dissemination throughout society. In the current situation, achieving widespread dissemination is especially important because it immediately translates into saved lives and economic progress. Diffusion is related to the issue of medication access in underdeveloped countries. Although rich economies create the majority of medical cures, they must be made available to the entire globe. This global policy viewpoint brings with it its own set of issues, which this study addresses in several areas.

Source: unido.org

In poor and middle-income countries that receive official development aid (ODA), innovation is becoming more important for a successful response to and recovery from the COVID-19 epidemic. On the one hand, incremental improvements to reuse current assistance programmes, and on the other, new biological and pharmaceutical product breakthroughs have dominated development and humanitarian responses to the epidemic. The majority of these activities stem from and are directed by players in high-income nations. There are few positive instances of innovations in poor and middle-income countries that take a more transformative, inclusive, and empowering approach, questioning established conventions and practises, and redefining the role of players. Such innovative activities may and should become more mainstream across the sector, both as a method of responding to COVID-19's immediate demands and as a means of reorienting the development and humanitarian sectors for the inevitable future difficulties.

How did we get up in this predicament?

Why don't we put more money into vaccine development?

More than forty healthcare businesses began researching COVID-19 vaccines as the seriousness of the epidemic became obvious. This increase in research funding will not change the reality that the first vaccination will not be available for at least another 18 months.

We could have been better prepared, according to the facts. Based on part of their work on SARS, another respiratory ailment, an American researcher recently told the US Congress that he and his colleagues were working on a vaccine against a strain of coronavirus in 2016. However, there was little interest in coronavirus research at the time, and he was unable to get the required money to continue his studies. The inadequacy of scientific resources committed to creating vaccinations was recently highlighted by the John Hopkins Center for Health Security a few months before the epidemic. It was arguing for the construction of a vaccination platform to bring all of the studies on the subject together. When there is an outbreak, governments and corporations are eager to invest heavily in vaccine development. However, when the outbreak fades, so does the attention of funders.

Vaccines, in contrast to many other 'products' of the pharmaceutical/ biomedical business, are subject to persistent underinvestment in R&D by private pharmaceutical corporations. The need for vaccinations and the intrinsic qualities of R&D are the two key factors.

In normal times, there isn't enough demand for immunizations.

Vaccines are often underutilised as a financial good. Consumer use is insufficient to encourage companies to invest in vaccine development. The fact that getting vaccinated has a 'positive externality' is one explanation for this underconsumption. Individuals who receive immunizations help not just themselves but also the rest of the population by breaking the cycle of disease transmission. As a result, not everyone needs to get vaccinated since they can ride on the backs of those who are, a notion known as herd immunity. Second, customers appear to be prepared to spend far more for therapy than for prevention. According to Kremer and Snyder, this practise pushes pharmaceutical corporations to spend research money on medications rather than vaccinations (2015). Third, many individuals in many nations do not think that vaccination is an effective way of protection, and many residents place little trust in government messages regarding vaccination's advantages.

All of these variables together result in a lower demand for vaccinations than one might expect for such a life-saving medication. Furthermore, because there is little demand, potential vaccine developers are unable to invest in R&D and large-scale manufacturing facilities.

In truth, just a few firms are working in this field. Novartis' significant vaccine division was sold to GSK in 2014 due to losses, leaving just GSK,

Merck, Sanofi, Pfizer, and Novavax as important participants in the vaccination industry.

Let us not be deceived. The absence of sufficient commercial demand for vaccinations does not imply that there is no need for them. Vaccines are in high demand, particularly in developing nations, where we know that outbreaks are linked to poverty and poor living circumstances (Snowden 2019). However, because the market sector is not profitable enough, big pharmaceutical corporations ignore this need for vaccinations.

What about the present economic downturn?

Faced with the grave scenario, several players have banded together to develop new ways to address the issues raised. Two new measures, in particular, incentivize firms to conduct more vaccine research, boost manufacturing capacity, and price vaccines fairly (i.e. close to production costs). On the one hand, public-private partnerships for vaccine development, and on the other, sophisticated market commitments such as research awards, are examples of these systems.

In the pharmaceutical industry, the traditional approach to innovation is to go through a lengthy process that begins with the discovery and generation of potential drug compounds and progresses through a meticulous refinement and selection phase before moving on to gradual development, clinical testing, and market approval. Although this paradigm will continue to be the most effective in drug development in the future, it is currently being supplemented by an ultrafast approach to innovation based on repurposing readily accessible ideas, information, and technology.

Source: blogs.insead.edu

During a Crisis, Innovation

Source: jnjinnovation.com

People throughout the world are still suffering from the health and economic effects of COVID19 a few months after the epidemic began. As the crisis progresses and scientists expect further

outbreaks, we must fight the natural inclination to escape to our safe havens to weather the storm. Instead, we must grab the potential for cross-sector research and technology cooperation to combat the illness while also implementing innovative digital health care solutions that our society desperately requires. We must adopt an urgent short-term plan to save lives, guided by research, but always with an eye on the long term.

This inventive approach will require a large pool of expertise. Although there is enough of research potential, the epidemic has forced many laboratories and teams to close and scatter. Although private funding tends to lean toward marketable solutions, crucial discoveries are more likely to arise from "why" questions (for example, fundamental research into the biology of the disease) rather than "shovel-ready" drug development programmes. Furthermore, brilliant ideas frequently emerge from unexpected places.

Outside of biology, useful solutions can be identified through engineering disciplines and information technology.

Covid-19 Response And Recovery Actors In Urban Governance

The COVID-19 circumstances have reminded us of the critical role of state capacity and public resources in ensuring the economic, social, and public health and biosecurity functions of cities. They have shed light on both the growing importance of urban municipalities in addressing complex challenges and the distributed nature of urban governance capacity across state and national government, private sector, philanthropic, not-for-profit, and community actors, as well as across spatialities that extend beyond the city's boundaries. City networks, private sector-led partnerships, philanthropies, and civic organisations are among four main sets of players whose goal has shifted toward urban governance innovations through COVID-19, operating through, alongside, and without reference to other state actors.

Most innovative systems rely on patents to function.

Patents have long been thought of as a stimulant for research and development. Knowledge is a 'public good,' as defined in Box 2, which means that it is impossible to prohibit others from using it and that its use by one person does not limit its availability to other prospective users. A particular piece of information often creates more advantages for society as a whole than a private player can obtain from its production and commercialization. As a result, economists believe that an innovator's incentives for developing new knowledge are suboptimal from the standpoint of society—and that the patent system is one approach to improve these incentives.

The pharmaceutical sector makes a strong argument for patent protection. Developing a novel medication is dangerous, time-consuming, and (very) costly. However, once a medicine's active ingredient has been found and tested, replicating it is typically simple, and manufacturing the drug is very inexpensive. As a result, few, if any, private enterprises would be involved in medication research without patent protection. Simply said, patent protection grants monopolistic power, which functions as a carrot to encourage companies to spend in R&D. Patent protection, on the other hand, is not a perfect incentive mechanism. Scholars have emphasised, among other things, that patent monopolies decrease access to pharmaceuticals by recovering research costs, and that market demand, rather than health requirements, influences research priorities (Barton and Emanuel 2005).

It's difficult to say if other incentive systems might be more effective than patent protection in promoting medical research. The scope of this paper does not allow for an answer to this question. Patent protection exists in the technological industry, and some players are scrambling to file patent applications. As a result, the many parties participating in the search for answers may mistakenly or intentionally infringe on patents that have been awarded.

Since the initial genomic sequence of the SARS-CoV-2 virus was disclosed in January, vaccine makers have been working at breakneck pace. Market failures matter a lot, as seen by the tremendous acceleration of public and private investment that we are seeing. Market failures for vaccine consumption have diminished for SARS-CoV-2, which is fortunate. Hundreds of millions, if not billions, of people want it, and a considerable portion of them are ready to pay more than the production cost. Furthermore, the majority of R&D-related commercial failures have vanished. Competition among nations to be the first to get new vaccines reduces the problem of free riders and enhances R&D incentives.

For years, analysts have highlighted that education and clinical care are two areas that have been largely unscathed by the disruptive developments that have revolutionised other industries such as banking, retail, and manufacturing.

Not because there was no need for transformational (rather than incremental) change, not because there were no innovative options available, not because leaders were unaware of the need, but because a slew of obstacles, ranging from payment to regulatory to the natural human aversion to change, all stymied the implementation of many innovations.

Ironically, a biologic agent, the COVID-19 virus, now appears to be the trigger for upheaval in educational and health care systems to a degree and at a rate previously unthinkable. While abstract tabletop exercises and apocalyptic works may have foreshadowed our current state of affairs, who among us imagined a pandemic in the near future? Innovations that have been accessible for years or decades but have not been widely adopted have now become the standard. However, the COVID-19 epidemic has uncovered flaws in the United States' health care system and underlined the need for further innovation. I briefly discuss a few instances of inventive answers, the directionality of needed future innovations, and their present and future consequences for AMCs, faculty, and educational programmes in this Invited Commentary.

Virtual Assistance

For decades, people have written about and studied the utility and value of technology-enabled, asynchronous in space and/or time virtual care, known as telemedicine. While cost, licensure, and privacy concerns were key roadblocks, several clinical systems, like as Kaiser Permanente, had already used virtual visits for the bulk of their ambulatory patient encounters prior to COVID-19. Kaiser, on the other hand, was an outlier. This has altered as a result of the epidemic. Virtual visit capabilities have been significantly increased across the United States, and in-person clinical appointments have been converted to virtual visits for a wide range of issues, from chronic illness follow-up to urgent care triaging. Individuals who are concerned about a possible COVID-19 infection should phone their physician's office rather than go to a clinic or emergency department for assessment, according to public service announcements.

Virtual visits, like many other advances, offer benefits and drawbacks. Convenience and access without the risk of further exposure are advantages for the patient. The capacity to care for patients with acute and chronic conditions while allowing patients to adhere to shelter-in-place rules and reducing health-care worker exposures are advantages for clinicians. Virtual visits also increase the availability of clinical resources for face-to-face encounters with patients who have been virtually screened and judged to require in-person visits, a process known as "forward triage."

Once the epidemic is over, it's likely that the monetary, regulatory, and privacy requirements that have permitted the inventive use of virtual visits will stay in place. What does the fact that telemedicine is still a standard-of-care option mean for academics, students, and AMCs? Video visits will be routine on a variety of platforms. While these are an improvement over audio-only conversations or email exchanges, the amount of information conveyed nonverbally remains minimal, the flow of conversation remains somewhat stilted, the social value of in-person interactions is absent, the opportunity for physical examination is obviously absent (unless the patient has been provided with specialised equipment), and the "healing touch" is impossible. In addition, therapists must understand the best practises for using video-based virtual communication technologies and create a "web side way."

For AMCs, virtual patient visits will demand changes to clinical faculty productivity and remuneration models based on relative value units. Telemedicine will necessitate the same level of education and training in the intricacies of virtual visits and the development of "web side manner" for students and residents as it does for traditional in-person patient interactions. Although some medical schools have created virtual communication exercises, this is still an area that has to be pushed further. Partnerships with academics from theatre, media arts, and broadcasting disciplines might provide a lot of benefits.

At-Home Hospital

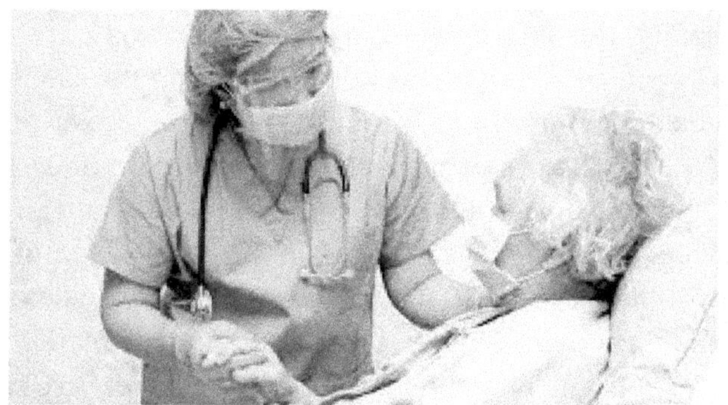

Source: healthaffairs.org

Not only has the pandemic resulted in widespread virtual visits and public education that people with COVID-19 symptoms should self-quarantine and treat themselves at home unless they are seriously ill, but it has also resulted in recommendations that people with COVID-19 symptoms self-quarantine and treat themselves at home. While the notion of a "hospital at home" has been examined and shown to be comparable to or superior than inpatient stays for a variety of diseases, despite worries about the rising prevalence of nosocomial infections and medical care costs, it has not been a first choice or alternative. Could the pandemic serve as a wake-up call for professionals and patients alike about the need of in-home care, even acute care? Sensors for a variety of physiologic variables with remote monitoring capabilities have been developed, albeit they are not yet commonly accessible outside of the hospital context. Could the need for alternate treatment settings as a result of hospital bed shortages lead to advancements that make hospital-at-home care the preferable option for all patients except those who are severely sick and require intensive care?

While many patients would welcome such a change, it would pose major financial concerns to AMCs, which rely heavily on inpatient clinical fees. Hospital-at-home care would need the development of new skills and the acceptance of new responsibilities for many faculty members.

Such care will necessitate not just virtual communication abilities but also the development of knowledge and skills to be sophisticated consumers of remote sensor data for both students and professors. Physicians and physicians-in-training, in particular, would need to learn how to recognise bogus or corrupted signals. The output of monitoring equipment is well-known to clinicians; the instruments in modern critical care units and operating rooms generate vast volumes of sensor data. It's simple to go to the patient's bedside and ascertain if a lead has been lost or gone out if an irregular ECG recording happens in the hospital. Remotely caring for patients, on the other hand, would involve different methods of verifying the authenticity of anomalous signals that, if verified, would compel intervention. Is it necessary for medical educators to collaborate with engineering academics to design creative courses and simulations to teach future physicians about the benefits and drawbacks of technology that will allow patients to be cared for at home and in other remote locations?

Diagnosis and Treatment Advances

The speed with which the COVID-19 genome was mapped, diagnostic tests devised and implemented, and treatment clinical trials began was astounding by historical standards. The rapidity with which these discoveries were made shows the revolutionary impact that a slew of scientific and technological breakthroughs may have on clinical practise. Medical instructors will benefit from the COVID-19 experience since it offers a variety of teaching alternatives that are universally relevant. While genomic-based assays appear to be quite reliable, they merely reflect the presence or absence of virus in the sample. Their sensitivity and specificity are determined by a variety of parameters, including the sufficiency of sample, transport medium, and the assay's technical limitations. Clinicians must still make decisions based on their patients‘ symptoms.

Individuals who first tested negative but were later revealed to be positive after possibly exposing a large number of additional people, as well as persons who tested positive but were clinically fundamentally healthy, have been reported in the media. While doctors appreciate the significance of technology in assisting diagnosis, the COVID-19 case highlights how even advanced diagnostic techniques must be used in conjunction with clinical judgement. The discovery of the virus in seemingly healthy people demonstrates the challenges and problems that physicians will confront when genetic screening becomes more widely available: What relevance does a discovery have for the individual? The proliferation of microbiome studies will further muddle the picture. Furthermore, the present epidemic demonstrates the ethical and professional dilemmas that doctors face when a seemingly healthy person tests positive for something—in this case, an infectious agent—that might damage others. What are the clinician's obligations to that person in terms of safeguarding the public's health? The famous case of "Typhoid Mary" exemplifies this issue as a current example of a long-standing problem.

Virtual Learning

While I've only touched on the ramifications of a few of the innovations that have evolved as a result of the COVID-19 pandemic's clinical necessities, schooling has also been disturbed, as I said earlier. In-person classes are being converted to virtual courses by faculty. Clinical rotations for medical students have been eliminated. Residents' clinical duties and educational opportunities have changed. The foundations of medical education have been shattered. This upheaval has also resulted in broad innovation, but it is less visible to the general public and the media. The promise of web-based education, like that of telemedicine, has been promoted for years, but acceptance among educational institutions has been uneven. The Khan Academy and the Human Diagnosis Project, for example, are effective examples of web-based instructional initiatives having worldwide reach. These exemplars serve as proof of concept, and medical school faculties are now being forced to transition their in-person training to virtual courses as a matter of necessity. Such advancements provide medical educators with a chance to use technology to create courseware that combines empirically generated insights into how people learn. Electronic educational materials and virtual courses offer many potential benefits, including frequent testing (i.e., the retrieval practise effect) with feedback, spaced learning and interleaving, a focus on threshold concepts, scaffolding, minimization of cognitive overload, and self-paced learning. This technology-mediated education, on the other hand, necessitates new skills and institutional infrastructure, as well as time and effort, as it entails more than merely recording a lecture and uploading slides. Could TED

(Technology, Entertainment, and Design) talk experts help medical educators? Professionals in the marketing field? From serious game developers?

Although these educational innovations, like other advancements, have a lot of promise, there are certain downsides to consider. What role do social interactions in medical school classrooms and laboratories have in professionalisation? Will we forego the potential for academics and students to form mentoring relationships? The possible harmful impact on professors, in particular, must be overlooked. Many of the core courses in medical school are the same from one institution to the next. The creation of a number of national or worldwide "superstar virtual educators" is a natural continuation of the growth of virtual courses, and it might abolish or drastically change the educational obligations of many present faculty members. Nonetheless, technology-enabled virtual learning may be a logical evolution of many schools‘ existing flipped classroom and hybrid classroom programmes, and instructors would still be needed to act as coaches, host and regulate online conversations, and offer feedback. Faculty members will continue to be needed, although their duties may change substantially.

Virtual Clinical Education

Medical students being removed from their clinical rotations is a major disruption. There are several ramifications for their ethical and professional growth as physicians.

Medical educators must act now, not just examine the ramifications, but quickly innovate and offer alternatives to fill the hole. Indeed, in response to the flood of creative ideas from AMC faculty, the Association of American Medical Colleges has created "a new free and open resource repository that will allow for the rapid sharing and distributing of these teaching techniques."

Simulated patients and simulation technology have already become commonplace in medical education. Simulated patients are used to teach communication and physical examination skills, and students and residents must demonstrate competency with simulated procedures before executing them real patients. The next frontier in educational programme creation is augmented and virtual reality. Could this technology, which is already being used to teach anatomy and surgical operations, be used to replace, at least in part, what trainees learnt on clinical rotations? Patient interviews for specific problems, illness presentations, and team training are just a few of the many uses for augmented and virtual reality instructional systems.

To take full advantage of these opportunities, medical educators must collaborate with video game makers, the military, and others working at the cutting edge of augmented and virtual reality. Importantly, while the new technology is intriguing, simulations can only augment rather than completely replace actual patient contacts in medical education. Medical educators must concentrate on implementing these cutting-edge technologies in areas where they bring value.

Important Decisions

The COVID-19 pandemic has altered the course of history. Academic medicine will evolve, as will the responsibilities of faculty, administrators, and students. We must make a choice as a group. Will AMC faculty and leaders, as well as regulators and accrediting agencies, embrace the innovations that this situation demands?

Will we make them permanent, embracing changes that are, in some cases, long needed, or will we just put up with them for the time being before returning to the pre-COVID-19 status quo? While we will mourn the loss of what was, I urge all of us to continue to tap into our faculties' inventive potential and improve our AMCs for the benefit of our students, patients, and society.

Conclusion

There is no doubt that virtual health care may give long-term access to necessary health care; nonetheless, the purpose of this opinion is to highlight the unanticipated health equity consequences of the shift to digital health care from the start of the current pandemic response. We don't have enough data to quantify these issues, which is one of the key limitations of our opinion. Measurement-based approaches to health equity, we feel, should be a top goal for digital health research.

The creation of drug(s) and vaccine(s) to help us overcome the current crisis is, understandably, the entire focus of attention these days. We looked at the conditions and methods, as well as the institutional and political frameworks, that could have aided their progress.

The immediate lessons in terms of science and innovation policy are harsh: lost time in research and technology cannot be made up. Furthermore, an aggressive but late mobilisation of resources focused at specific scientific goals would not compensate for the insufficiency of private investments and incorrect public policy measures that have defined recent vaccine R&D efforts. Economic theories like market failures (and their cures) and the application of notions like the elasticity of science, it appears to us, provide significant instruments for contemplating on STI policy concerns that typify times of crisis and enormous social challenges. The current report is a first step in that direction. However, in terms of STI policy, the evaluation and prospects of the crisis must be restricted to this urgent and compelling hunt for vaccines and other important technologies. Our civilization need more than technology remedies to avert epidemics (ex-ante) or alleviate their repercussions (ex-post). A precautionary second line of defence asks for the creation of knowledge of a different sort than what the first line of defence will create. It entails the creation of specialised types of technical and organisational competence for ex-ante and ex-post responses to probable pandemics, as well as public health education and infrastructure. This reaction refers to a wide variety of research and innovation initiatives that span (and combine) numerous disciplines and allow society to organise and enlighten itself collectively in order to cope with forced adjustments in order to avoid and respond to pandemics.

The current situation serves as a reminder that science in all of its forms is important. As a society, we must deal with all aspects of the pandemic, which necessitates the use of all scientific fields. For example, we believe that economic knowledge is essential for reducing the pandemic's consequences and comprehending the economic processes that have led to the current situation in order to propose improvements. Other domains of social and behavioural sciences, on the other hand, are proving to be equally important in maximising pandemic response.

However, the true and severe impact of this crisis on innovation may be seen at a higher level than that which has been explored thus far. The system itself may evolve, in what Nobel Laureate economist Paul Romer refers to as "innovations in meta-rules," or "the rules for changing rules." 'Stable systems of rules (or meta-rules) are difficult to modify, even when the environment changes and they are no longer ideal, since reaching consensus and coordinating change is exceedingly costly and complex,' he adds (Romer 2010). The shock of the crisis will undoubtedly aid us in changing some of these regulations. The current crisis has shook up the whole STI ecology, providing a chance to question traditional standards. In the realm of innovation, the impact of the crisis will most likely be seen at this level. Consider disruptions of meta-rules in the spatial arrangement of work or even leisure activities—disruptions that we are already witnessing can, in turn, lead to other highly important changes. Following the economic shock that industries like low-cost airlines will face, one specific example is the sustainable transportation arena. In the sphere of medical technology, let us also note breakthroughs in meta-rules relating to health infrastructures and their operation, geographical dispersion, and international coordination of supply chains. Finally, let us discuss the changes that will occur in terms of science organisation, knowledge sharing, and data sharing.

These three examples of rule modifications, which would be impossible to implement in normal times, demonstrate the significant progress that may be made in these areas—and this could be viewed as a good influence on society.

This beneficial effect is less clear, and it has to be examined in terms of legal and privacy regulation changes that the proliferation of electronic tracking and identifying technology may bring about. The future is bright, and ensuring that COVID-related health system innovation is sustained will undoubtedly add a glimmer.

References

- J.O. Woolliscroft, J. O. Woolliscroft, J. O. Woollis (2020). Innovating in the face of the COVID-19 epidemic. Academic Medicine is a term that refers to the practise of
- G. Abi Younes, C. Ayoubi, O. Ballester, G. Cristelli, G. de Rassenfosse, G. Foray, D. Foray, D. Foray, D. Foray, D. Foray, D. Foray, D. Foray, D. Foray, D. Foray, D. Foray, D. Foray, D. Foray, D. Foray (2020). COVID-19: Innovation Economists' Perspectives 733-745 in Science and Public Policy, vol. 47, no. 5.
- E. A. Samuels, S. A. Clark, C. Wunsch, L. A. J. Keeler, N. Reddy, R. Vanjani, and R. S. Wightman (2020). During COVID-19, there will be a focus on improving access to addiction treatment. The Journal of Addiction Medicine is a publication dedicated to the study of addiction.
- G. Farrugia and R. W. Plutowski (2020, August). The COVID-19 epidemic taught us a lot about innovation. Proceedings of the Mayo Clinic (Vol. 95, No. 8, p. 1574). Elsevier.
- P. Azoulay and B. Jones (2020). COVID-19 must be defeated by ingenuity. Science, vol. 368, no. 6491, pp. 553-553.
- P. McGuirk, R. Dowling, S. Maalsen, and T. Baker (2021). COVID19 and urban governance innovation 188-195 in Geographical Research, vol. 59, no. 2.
- G. Von Krogh, B. Kucukkeles, and S. M. Ben-Menahem (2020). The COVID-19 epidemic taught us a lot about quick innovation. 8-10 in MIT

Sloan Management Review, vol. 61, no. 4.

- A. Crawford and E. Serhal (2020). COVID-19 and digital health equity: the innovation curve cannot strengthen the health social gradient. e19361, Journal of medical Internet research, 22(6).
- R. Wynne, A. Conway, and P. M. Davidson (2021). Assuring the continuation of COVID-related innovation. 77(6), e4 in Journal of Advanced Nursing.
- B. Ramalingam and J. Prabhu (2020). COVID-19, innovation, and development: Challenges, Opportunities, and Next Steps 1-14 in OECD's Tackling Coronavirus (COVID-19): Contributing to a Global Effort.

CHAPTER THIRTEEN

Covid-19 Variants: Alpha Beta Delta And Omicron

-----**Jakir Ali Kazi*

Introduction

The virus, which was found in China's Wuhan province in 2019, should have been called the Wuhan virus, according to custom. But that name was not given. The name was given on its shape. Because the virus had a spike on it, it was named 'Corona' because it looked like a crown. The crown is that kings wear on their heads. Nowadays the Queen of England is seen wearing such a crown. Then the name is not according to the place but according to the shape. So, when a new species of coronavirus was found in the UK, it was given the name Alpha variant without the name Uk virus. Similarly, the virus found in South Africa is called the Beta variant, and the species found in Brazil is called Gama. Our India is not far behind in making variants. The second wave of Corona started in India, which was very terrible. Although there is debate as to whether this new variant is really created in India.

However, the death toll continued to rise sharply. Scientists have discovered that it is a new species of covid virus. That is why the species found in India was named the Delta variant. In this way, the new species currently found in South Africa is the Omicron variant. However, according to reports so far, the Delta variant is the deadliest.

Objectives:

1. From this article we will get a general idea about covid-19.
2. To know about SARS Virus.
3. Different variants of covid 19 can be learned.
4. It is possible to know how much influence a variant has had.
5. At the end of the lesson, we will know how important it is to think about covid-19.

Covid-19: the first thing you need to understand that Coronavirus is not the same name of a single virus. The name coronavirus has been assigned to a family of viruses. The common cold – cough that you catch during winters that too, is a type of coronavirus. In 2002-2003, a SARS virus had become widespread that too, was a type of coronavirus. And what is affecting people right now is a type of coronavirus. There's a place in china called Wuhan, it was found there on 31st December 2019. This new strain of coronavirus has been named N-COV, Novel Coronavirus. Novel means new. This strain is so now that they could not even think of a new. So, they named it Novel Coronavirus. The new Coronavirus looks somewhat like crown shape and in Latin crown pronounced at corona. WHO designed the name of the virus SARS -COV-2. Covid-19 is the name of the respiratory disease caused by SARS-COV-2.

The original source of most of the coronaviruses is mostly some animal which affects a human and then later through human to human contact. And through human-to-human transmission, these coronaviruses spread amongst humans. For example, in the case of SARS, the original source was a bat. MERS is another similar coronavirus that spread the middle east during 2012-2013, the original source of that was a camel. The exact original source of the new Coronavirus has not yet been discovered. Some scientists suspect that the original source might be snakes. But some scientists believe that they might be bats again because there are 90% similarities in the new Coronavirus as compared to the Coronavirus that came from bats.

What is a Variant? : In microbiology and virology, the term variant or "genetic variant" is used to describe a subtype of a microorganism that is genetically distinct from the main strain, but not sufficiently different to be termed a distinct strain. It was said in 2013 that "there is no universally accepted definition for the terms 'strain', 'variant', and 'isolate' in the virology community, and most virologists simply copy the usage of terms from others. The lack of precise definition continued in 2020; in the context of the Variant of Concern 202012/01 version of the SARS-CoV-2 virus, the website of the US Centers for Disease Control and Prevention (CDC) states, "For the time being in the context of this variant, the [terms "variant", "strain", and lineage"] are generally being used interchangeably by the scientific community".

Alpha Variant: Its original name is B.1.1.7. The first case was likely in mid-September 2020 in London or Kent, United Kingdom. The variant is known by several names. Outside the UK it is sometimes referred to as the UK variant or British variant or English variant, despite the existence of other, less common, variants first identified in the UK, such as the Eta variant (lineage B.1.525). Within the UK, it is commonly referred to as the Kent variant after Kent, where the variant was found. It is the first corona variant to be rapidly transmitted to humans. It proved to be the most influential virus in America. It is contagious to the original virus. According to the CDC(Centers for Disease Control and Prevention -is the national public health agency of the United States. It is a United States federal agency, under the Department of Health and Human Services) report, it is 66% more likely to be infected than the original virus. More people are being hospitalized with this species and its lethality is much higher than that of the original virus. However, the CDC said the vaccine could prevent the virus.

Beta variant: Original name B.1.351 The virus could be detected in South Africa by the end of 2020. The virus later spread around the world. However, the spread of the virus in the United States is much lower. It is 50% more contagious than the original virus. There is evidence that the Beta variant can cause more patient hospitalization and death than other forms. On 4 January 2021, UK newspaper The Telegraph reported that Oxford immunologist Sir John Bell believed there was "a big question mark" over the new South African variant's potential resistance to COVID-19 vaccines, raising fears that vaccines might not work as effectively on that variant strain. South Africa stopped taking Oxford–AstraZeneca Vaccine in early 2021, when clinical trails showed it did not provide strong protection against mild and moderate disease from the Beta Variant. Researchers and officials reported that the prevalence of the variant was higher among young people with no underlying health conditions, and more frequently causes serious illness in such cases than other variants. The South African health department also indicated that the variant may be driving the second wave of the COVID-19 pandemic in the country, as the variant spreads faster than other earlier variants of the virus.

Delta Variant: we will discuss this variant deeply because this virus is dominant in India. The World Health Organization has recently declared variant B.1.617.2 as 'Delta'. To avoid confusion, the species was formerly known as the Indian species, or 'Double Mutant'. The Kent variant in Britain is called Alpha, the Beta Variant in South Africa and Gamma in Brazil. Although there is no scientific evidence, physicians believe that the Delta

Variant is responsible for the second wave surge. As well as not following the covid-19 rules properly and starting the unlock process everywhere at once is also one of the reasons for the increase in infection. However, as a result of the delta variant, many new symptoms have been seen this year. Many of which are deadly enough. As a result, many people had to be hospitalized, even had to stay in the ICU. This new variant is much more contagious. Spikes can attack different cells of the human body by changing the size of the protein very quickly. And just as quickly, the human body's cells are weakened and spread to different parts of the body.

Some major symptoms of the Delta variant are as follows-

1. Stomach problems: Some stomach problems like diarrhea, abdominal pain, the tendency to vomit, loss of appetite, indigestion have been suffering from covid patients for a long time. Even after Covid has recovered, its impact has been going on for a long time.

2. Blood clots: Examples of blood clots have been found in many people this time. In many cases, a blood thinner has to be used. In some cases, blood clots form in the tissues and cause gangrene.

3. Lung damage: Sudden decrease in oxygen level in the blood. He has to be admitted to the hospital due to severe damage to his lungs. Loved ones are running for oxygen. This picture has become very familiar to everyone in the second wave. Many people have also suffered from various heart diseases due to lung damage.

4. Skin problems: Blackening of nails, various types of rashes, infections, hair loss and other skin problems have come up in the symptoms this time. Complaints of rash due to covid, especially among children, have been heard a lot.

5. Hearing loss: Many people complain that they are not able to hear properly after covid. According to experts, this symptom is actually the delta species.

Delta Plus: Researchers say the Indian variant of the coronavirus, which has long been called the 'Delta' variant, has changed to a second phase. The variant, which was first identified in Europe, is being dubbed as 'Delta Plus'.Citing several studies, the Indian Ministry of Health says that the so-called 'Delta Plus' variant spreads more easily than previous variants, attaches more easily to lung cells and the vaccine used to prevent coronavirus is based on the principle - 'against monoclonal antibody therapy. This new variant is related to the 'Delta' variant identified in India. Delta variant is thought to be the main reason behind the second outbreak of coronavirus in India. The Indian Ministry of Health says that the first Delta Plus variant was made available in India in April this year. This variant has been found in 6 districts of three states. Apart from India, this Delta Plus variant has been found in 9 countries including the United States, United Kingdom, Russia, and China. On the other hand, the Delta variant has already spread to 70 countries around the world.Viruses usually change all the time. In many cases the virus changes and becomes weak. In some cases, the mutated virus appears to be stronger and more contagious than the older virus, which makes the mutation more deadly than other variants.

The Delta Plus variant has an additional mutation called 'K417N', which is also found in beta and gamma variants identified in South Africa and Brazil.

Omicron variant: Corona's new strain Omicron shows its dominance all over the world. The infection has spread at lightning speed in India as well. According to some public health experts, the third wave of corona has already started in India. However, this new wave is different from the previous two waves. Everyone who is affected by the doctor is accepting it in one word. Let's take a look at how different this new strain of corona is from the first two waves. People affected by the first wave of corona had no taste or smell. At least not for the first seven days. There was a dry cough. However, the cold did not last long. A CT scan of the victim's chest revealed the presence of covid jelly. Body temperature was quite high. The weakness of the affected person would be severe. People with co-morbidity had the most difficulty breathing. Among coronary heart disease patients, 10 percent were hospitalized. The number of casualties was also eye-catching. During the second wave, we saw that the taste or smell of the affected people was sometimes completely or partially gone. However, the cold did not last long. In this case also the presence of covid jelly could be found on the chest. At this stage there was fever for a long time. And almost all patients had respiratory problems. The number of hospital admissions is about 12 percent. Omicron virus, on the other hand, spreads rapidly, but there are no symptoms such as loss of taste or smell. The body temperature is not rising too much. No covid jelly was found on the chest of the victim. Symptoms such as nausea, mild fever, sore throat and headache have also been reported in some of the Omicron sufferers. The tendency to be hospitalized is also much lower. According to the World Health Organization, Omicron's attack is far less effective than the previous two waves due to the effectiveness of the vaccine. Health experts believe that India is fighting a third wave, relying on the character of the virus in general and overall vaccination. Many experts and the World Health Organization have hinted that the end of the coronavirus is likely to begin in 2022.

Present scenario : The current variant of corona virus is called Omicron. The Omicron variant was being assumed to be a mild variant. That's mean it is a less threatening variant as compared to the Delta variant. Delta variant was the variant because of which we witnessed the deadly second wave in India. Then it was an assumption of the scientists and experts l. But now several studies have been published by a various research group in various countries that prove this is not a threatening variant. The first study was from the University of Edinburgh. Edinburgh is the capital of Scotland. They had used the national surveillance data to compare Omicron and Delta infection. They found that the risk of hospitalisation due to the Omicron variant was 65% lower than that the Delta variant. The chief medical advisor of the president of the USA said that the Omicron variant is almost unstoppable. Irrespective of how hard you try to stop, it would not be stopped. It will infect a lot of people and everyone will eventually be through this. Because it is so highly transmissible. Dr. Jaiprokash said the same thing. He is the chairperson of scientific advisory committee at the Indian council of medical research. And it was not a bad news because according to him, the majority of people wouldn't even know that they were inflected. It is being believed that 80% of people will get inflected but they will be unaware of it. B it will be so mild.

References :

- "South Africa announces a new coronavirus variant". The New York Times. 18 December 2020. https://nytimes.com
- Wikipedia,(2021),"variant(biology)"https://en.m.wikipedia.org/wiki/Variant_(biology)
- Wikipedia (2021), https://en.m.Wikipedia.org
- Higgins-Dunn, N. (19 December 2020). "The U.K. has identified a new Covid-19 strain that spreads more quickly. Here's what they know". MSNBC.
- Peacock, Sharon (22 December 2020). "Here's what we know about the new variant of coronavirus". The Guardian.
- Mkhize, Dr Zwelini (18 December 2020). "Update on Covid-19 (18th December 2020)" (Press release). South Africa. COVID-19 South

African Online Portal. Retrieved 23 December 2020.

- “Q&A on coronaviruses (COVID-19)”. World Health Organization (WHO). 17 April 2020.
- Dr. Prokash, Jay : “Everyone Will Get Omicron, Boosters Won’t Stop It”(2022) https://ndtv.com
- The University of Edinburgh (2021) “Delta variant impact on hospitalisation revealed”. https://ed.ac.uk
- “Symptoms of Coronavirus”. U.S. Centers for Disease Control and Prevention (CDC). 13 May 2020.
- COVID-19 vaccines”. World Health Organization (WHO). 3 March 2021.
- Knapton, Sarah (4 January 2021). “South African variant may evade vaccines and testing, warn scientists”. www.telegraph.co.uk.
- “2nd U.S. Case Of Wuhan Coronavirus Confirmed”. https://NPR.org. NPR. 4 April 2020
- Novel corona virus(PDF). World Health Organization (WHO). 21 January 2020.
- “B.1.1.7 report”. https://Cov-lineages.org. 29 January 2021.
- Public Health England (16 February 2021). “Variants: distribution of cases data”. https://Gov.UK.
- Roberts, Michelle (2 February 2021). “UK variant has mutated again, scientists say”. BBC News.

CHAPTER FOURTEEN

Covid Vaccine Plan Of India

------* **Dr. Ekata Gupta***Divine Tomar*****Nilesh Kumar Dokania**

Introduction

The first case of new coronavirus infections was discovered a year ago in China's Wuhan province. Efforts were focused on avoiding and reducing transmission during the early stages of the disease. COVID-19 vaccinations that are effective are urgently needed, according to a global review of herd immunity. Coronavirus disease 2019 (COVID-19) is the most serious public health threat of the twenty-first century, affecting millions of individuals around the world. Due to the lack of a broad and effective treatment for COVID-19 or a prevention strategy for SARS-CoV-2 dissemination, the outbreak of severe acute respiratory syndrome coronavirus 2 (SARS-CoV-2) has sparked an unprecedented effort from the scientific community in the development of new vaccines on various platforms.

In India, free immunization against COVID-19 began on January 16, 2021, and the government is asking all of its inhabitants to get vaccinated as part of what is likely to be the world's largest vaccination programme. Four of the eight COVID-19 vaccines currently undergoing clinical trials in India were created there. Covishield (the Oxford-AstraZeneca vaccine) and Covaxin, a home-grown vaccine produced by Bharat Biotech, have been licenced for limited emergency use by India's medicines authority. Manufacturers in India have said that they will be able to meet the country's future COVID-19 vaccination needs. The workforce and cold-chain infrastructure in place prior to the pandemic are sufficient to vaccinate 30 million healthcare workers in the first instance.

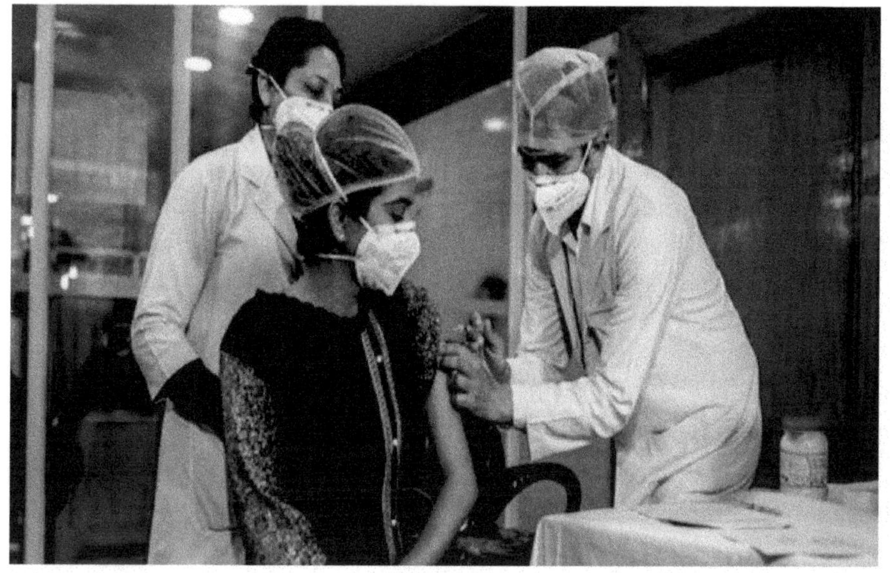

Source: www.news18.com

The Indian government has taken immediate steps to increase the country's vaccine manufacturing capacity, as well as a computerised system to address and monitor all elements of vaccine administration. Despite the fact that the vaccine is not necessary, India, which has a population of 1380 million people (as of 2020), plans to give it to all of its residents who are willing to take it. Due to India's large population, vaccine importation may not be the best solution. According to the International Air Transport Association (IATA), transporting the vaccine from production sites abroad to distribution areas would necessitate thousands of flights.

India, which has a sophisticated vaccine development programme, intends to manufacture COVID-19 vaccine domestically as well as distribute it to countries that cannot afford to acquire expensive vaccines from the West. COVID-19 vaccine candidates in development and clinical testing in India are among the most advanced products in the world. Apart from the COVID-19 vaccines developed in India, other local pharmaceutical and biotech companies have inked collaboration agreements with vaccine developers from other countries. These cooperation vary from clinical trials through vaccine manufacture and distribution on a wide scale. The following is a list of eight vaccine candidates that are currently being tested in India.

Oxford-AstraZeneca, Codagenix, and Novavax have all struck agreements with the Serum Institute of India (SII) in Pune. It is now mass-producing the Oxford-AstraZeneca Adenovirus vector-based vaccine AZD1222 (also known as "Covishield" in India), and it has roughly 50 million doses on hand. SII plans to increase its capacity to 2 billion doses per year. The Drugs Controller General of India (DCGI) and the Indian Council for Medical Research have granted Covishield a "at-risk manufacturing and stockpiling licence" (ICMR). The ICMR funded the clinical trials of the Covishield vaccine developed with the master stock from Oxford-AstraZeneca. The US-based pharma claims that their Covid jab was found to be 89.3% effective in a UK trial.

One of the company's two vaccines is CovaxinTM, India's first indigenous COVID-19 vaccine, developed and manufactured by Bharat Biotech International Limited in conjunction with the National Institute of Virology of the ICMR. CovaxinTM is a virus vaccine that was created in Vero cells. As an adjuvant, the inactivated virus is mixed with Alhydroxiquim-II (Algel-IMDG), a chemosorbed imidazoquinoline onto aluminum hydroxide gel that boosts immune response and provides longer-lasting immunity. A licensing arrangement with Kansas-based ViroVax allows this technology to be deployed.

India has enough capacity to produce vaccines (about 2.4 billion doses per year) as well as medical and surgical disposables such vials, stoppers, syringes, gauze, and alcohol swabs. The obstacle, however, was the vaccine storage and shipment, which had very particular temperature regimens. Some vaccines being developed and manufactured in other regions of the world require storage temperatures as low as 80 degrees Celsius. Fortunately, the vaccines that India was the first to launch for distribution only require a storage temperature of 2–8 °C. The government has been working on strategies to ensure that the COVID-19 vaccination is distributed quickly and effectively. Vaccine producers have begun airlifting vaccines in cold boxes with digital temperature tags to four large depots in Haryana, Mumbai, Chennai, and Kolkata, where they will be housed in walk-in coolers. The vaccines would then be sent to selected stores in 37 states/UTs by flights or insulated vans. The State/UT administrations transport them from these 41 centres to temperature-controlled facilities at district-level vaccination depots. Vaccines are kept in ice-lined refrigerators

(ILRs) in districts, then transferred to distribution facilities in cold boxes and ultimately to vaccination sites in ice-packed vaccine carriers. The COVID Vaccine Intelligence Network (Co-WIN) vaccine delivery management system, which is a cloud-based digitalized platform, already monitors the temperature of 29,000 cold-chain locations in real-time. The Co-WIN platform was created in India, but it can be used by any country. For this, the Indian government will provide help.

Pfizer India is said to have requested extra time, but the company's mRNA vaccine has already been approved for emergency use in a number of nations, including the United States and the United Kingdom, as well as by the World Health Organization (WHO). Though the extraordinarily low temperature of 70°C required for storing the Pfizer vaccine makes delivery in India difficult, the company has indicated that it will make the appropriate accommodations. However, current Indian rules prohibit the use of any vaccination (such as the Pfizer vaccine) that has not passed adequate clinical testing in India.

The Indian government has established a National Expert Group on COVID-19 Vaccine Administration (NEGVAC) to advise on all aspects of COVID-19 vaccine administration in India19. The COVID-19 vaccination will be administered initially to healthcare workers, frontline workers, and people over 50 (with a preference for those over 60), followed by people under 50 with comorbidities. The government has formed a group of experts from numerous specialities, including oncology, nephrology, pulmonology, and cardiology, to determine the clinical criteria that should be used to prioritise persons with comorbidities for Covid-19 vaccination. After providing some confirmation of identity, eligible persons who have been missed from the rolls for one reason or another will be able to self-register for vaccination. The remaining population will be vaccinated based on disease epidemiology and vaccine availability after over 300 million people were vaccinated in the first wave.

The Indian government has arranged for 600 million doses of the COVID-19 vaccine to be procured from the above-mentioned firms, and is in the process of negotiating for another billion doses. The government bought Covishield, developed by SII, and Covaxin, produced by Bharat Biotech Ltd, and these were first administered. Nonetheless, as and when the other vaccinations are licenced for delivery after clinical trials, the government may change its strategy.

How centres may be laid out

HT

Each centre will need to have three separate rooms, Centre has suggested

1 WAITING ROOM/AREA

- This is where people – who will be given slots – will have their identities authenticated and verified

- People will need to be seated in a socially distant manner, and the area would have hand washing/sanitising facility

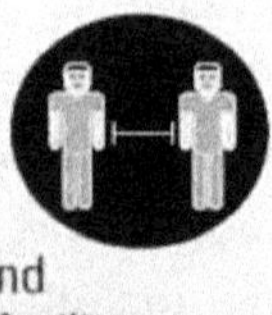

2 VACCINATION ROOM

- This is where the dose will be given and only one person will be allowed here at a time

- If it is being administered to a woman, a female staff member must be present

3 OBSERVATION ROOM

- Once given a dose, people will move to this room and wait for 30 minutes to monitor for any immediate adverse reaction

- Here too people will need to sit at a distance from each other

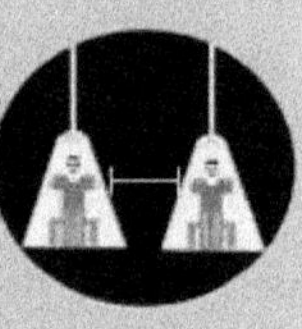

Source: www.hindustantimes.com

While obtaining the vaccine is the first step, distributing and immunizing the vast Indian population is a major logistical challenge. On November 24, 2020, Indian Prime Minister Shri Narendra Modi met with chief ministers and other representatives from states and union territories to discuss vaccination distribution strategy (UTs). On November 28, 2020, he paid a visit to the three major enterprises to get firsthand knowledge and to assure them of the government's complete support.

Midwives and auxiliary nurse midwives, who have a significantly broader reach in the interiors and rural areas, were included in the first group of health workers educated in vaccination capabilities, since India plans to have COVID-19 immunization campaigns in both urban and rural areas at the same time. These well-trained personnel will play a critical role in rural India's health care. The government intends to enlist the help of allied healthcare professionals such as pharmacists and public health officials in order to broaden a vaccination programme.

Not just in metropolitan areas, but also in rural areas of India, a considerable number of private clinical laboratories, including diagnostic laboratories, have been established. The majority of them have adequate infrastructure and people. Both the government and private clinical laboratories would benefit if they were included in the COVID-19 vaccine programme. All of these activities will be carried out under stringent regulatory oversight, with a standard operating procedure (SOP) to guide the trained workers and a standard protocol set by government bodies.

Conclusion

India is in a unique position to provide the globe with affordable medical, surgical, and vital generic medications. India is also well-known for being the world's largest vaccine production and distributor. The present COVID-19 pandemic has resulted in quick development, emergency use authorization, and unprecedented collaboration among numerous parties. Vaccination may be a cost-effective method for people's survival and a higher quality of life, as well as for the resuscitation of India's economy.

References

- Krause, P., Fleming, T. R., Longini, I., Henao-Restrepo, A. M., Peto, R., Dean, N. E., ... & Henao-Restrepo, A. M. (2020). COVID-19 vaccine trials should seek worthwhile efficacy. The Lancet, 396(10253), 741-743.
- Kochhar, S., & Salmon, D. A. (2020). Planning for COVID-19 vaccines safety surveillance. Vaccine, 38(40), 6194-6198.
- https://vaccine.icmr.org.in/covid-19-vaccine
- Le, T. T., Cramer, J. P., Chen, R., & Mayhew, S. (2020). Evolution of the COVID-19 vaccine development landscape. Nat Rev Drug Discov, 19(10), 667-668.
- Gupta, I., & Baru, R. (2020). Economics & ethics of the COVID-19 vaccine: How prepared are we?. The Indian Journal of Medical Research, 152(1-2), 153.
- Rego, G. N., Nucci, M. P., Alves, A. H., Oliveira, F. A., Marti, L. C., Nucci, L. P., ... & Gamarra, L. F. (2020). Current clinical trials protocols and the global effort for immunization against SARS-CoV-2. Vaccines, 8(3), 474.

- Wolemonwu, V. C. (2020). Human Challenge Trials for a COVID-19 Vaccine. Voices in Bioethics, 6.
- Kumar, V. M., Pandi-Perumal, S. R., Trakht, I., & Thyagarajan, S. P. (2021). Strategy for COVID-19 vaccination in India: the country with the second highest population and number of cases. Npj Vaccines, 6(1), 1-7.

CHAPTER FIFTEEN

New Way of Innovating India Digitally: "Make In India" During Covid 19

-----**Dr.Mukta Goyal*

Introduction

The most important factors are the country's development, prosperity, and success. India is regarded as one of the most powerful countries in the world, competing on an international basis in all fields.

In the response to the COVID-19 pandemic, necessity has been the mother of invention, and nowhere is this more evident than in India. Here's how frugal Indian innovations have taken the commercial route to aid the fight against the pandemic, with a clear focus on affordability and low cost.

The rapid innovation at the heart of India's response to the coronavirus pandemic has been a testament to its age-old tradition of being creative and resourceful in the face of social crisis and resource constraints, from sanitization drones, digital stethoscopes, and infection-proof fabric for hospitals to incredibly cheap portable ventilators and affordable Covid-19 test kits. With Indian Institutes of Technology (IITs) across the country spearheading the majority of these innovations, it's also a vote of confidence in the country's robust culture of practical innovation, which has always given the Indian economy an edge. During this time, key innovations were commercialised either through IIT-incubated startups or by the institutes awarding licenses to companies while keeping the patent rights.

India has an ideal, strong, and valuable climate, as well as optimal human and natural capital. Small and medium-sized businesses in India will help the nation take the next major step forward in manufacturing. For these industries, India should place a greater emphasis on novelty and creativity. The government must devise strategies to provide unique benefits and rights to these industries. India should also be prepared to address factors that have a negative impact on manufacturing productivity. India must maintain its power in order to keep up with China's dominance in the manufacturing sector.

The Honble Prime Minister launched the Make in India program.Mr. Modi in September 2014 as part of a broader set of nation-building initiatives.The program's goal is to turn India into a global design and manufacturing hub.

Make in India

Trade and investment have been disrupted as a result of the Covid-19 pandemic, particularly in sectors such as tourism and manufacturing. Unprecedented global economic downturns are on the horizon. Over-reliance on Chinese manufacturing, particularly in these difficult times, is hurting the global economy, as China accounts for 12% of global GDP growth. Global investors are shifting their manufacturing activities to India, Bangladesh, Thailand, and Vietnam as a result of the US-China trade war and strained diplomatic relations with China over the Covid-19 crisis. In this context, the pandemic could be used to turn India into a manufacturing hub and expand its export base, which could be realised through India's flagship 'Make in India' initiative.

Make in India is a global marketing campaigning slogan coined by Prime Minister Narendra Modi to attract foreign and domestic firms to produce their goods in India as a key investment destination and a global centre for production, architecture, and innovation. The campaign aims to entice multinational companies to set up manufacturing operations in India and to draw more foreign investment. The campaign's goal is to get the manufacturing industry to expand at a rate of more than 100% on a long-term basis. The government would examine all regulatory mechanisms in order to relieve taxpayers of their pressure.

Digital India is a multi-pronged initiative that spans multiple departments. This initiative will ensure that government services and information are available anywhere, at any time, on any device that is user-friendly and secure. With the Digital India project, the government is preparing for the large program by connecting every service with e-power.

The goal of Digital India is to make digital services available in Indian languages. The Digital India initiative could aid in the achievement of the

following goals:

- Education for all.
- Information for everyone.
- Universal access to broadband.
- The structure of leadership.

A dedicated cell has been established to reply to requests from business entities through a fresh developed net portal. The Union Government hopes that this movement can dispel the discouraging image of India's official bureaucratic procedure and sophisticated laws. It'd create it easier for world investors to form higher investment selections. This might create it easier to realize the goal of a liberalised economy. Create in India can function a key resource for international investors seeking steering on all sides of regulative and policy problems, furthermore as helping them in getting regulative clearances. The government's initiative can focus on developing physical infrastructure furthermore as establishing a digital network so as to rework India into a worldwide hub for producing products starting from cars to satellites to warships, prescribed drugs to ports, and paper to electricity. The Indian government has listed twenty-five target sectors for the create in India initiative that may be properly promoted.

For the past two decades, India's growth appears to have been led by the services sector. In the short term, this strategy paid off, and India's IT and BPO sectors boomed, earning the country the moniker of "world's back office." Despite the fact that the services sector's share of the Indian economy increased to 57 percent in 2013, it only accounted for 28 percent of employment in 2013. As a result, in order to increase employment, the manufacturing sector needed to be expanded. This is due to the services sector's current low absorption potential in relation to the country's demographic dividend.

Impact of COVID-19 on Make in India

China's handling of the COVID-19 pandemic has fuelled anti-Chinese sentiment while also affecting trade relations with the country. The global reliance on raw materials and made-in-China goods has been enormous, and countries are now reconsidering their trade relations with China.

China's GDP has averaged around 10% per year since 1978, when it first began reforming its economy. According to World Bank data from 2018, China's GDP increased by $14 trillion in 2018, an increase of more than $2 trillion over 2017. All of this, however, could change. The fear psychosis that has gripped the world as a result of China's handling of the COVID-19 pandemic has resulted in a number of events, including the United States, refusing to accept shipments from China into its ports.

India revised its FDI policy to eliminate takeovers or acquisitions of Indian companies aimed solely at the Chinese market. The purchase of shares in a major private sector bank in India by Chinese investors is a case in point. India's orders for 'faulty' rapid COVID-19 test kits were also cancelled. India's GDP is expected to grow at 1.9 percent in FY2021, making it the only other economy to grow besides China. A lot of its expansion could be due to a post-COVID-19 world with more opportunities.

India is not only a large market for investors, but it is also a viable place to do business, with a population of 1.3 billion people, more than 60% of whom are under the age of 25, a cheap workforce, and a strong democracy. Even though the ease of doing business in India has improved in recent years, it remains a complex ecosystem, which does not diminish the importance of India's infrastructure, which is still severely lacking. These elements have the potential to wreak havoc. Because of its large working-age population, it is also a desirable destination in the medium to long term. The Indian government has been announcing new incentives aimed at making India a more appealing investment destination for manufacturing firms.

A thorough review of import duties with the goal of encouraging manufacturing, a deep cut in the corporate tax rate to 22% for existing companies and 15% for new ones, and an import duty hike on a variety of products, from footwear and furniture to electrical appliances and toys, are just a few of the measures taken to help the industries in the February 1 budget for 2020-21.

The government unveiled a Rs 20 lakh crore stimulus package that included tax breaks for small businesses and incentives for domestic manufacturing. MSMEs will benefit from the Rs 3 lakh crore in collateral-free assistance given to them.

This move could aid India's factory output recovery, which fell to record lows in March, with the Index of Industrial Production contracting 16.7%. According to records, manufacturing output decreased by 20% in March, while electricity generation decreased by nearly 7%. In March, production in all categories of manufacturing industries fell, with the auto (50 percent decline) and computer & electronic products sectors being the worst hit (fell almost 42 percent).

Rather than being limited to just a producer for domestic markets, India has enormous potential as an additional export base. China's rising wages have compelled global value chains to look for new markets. For the first time in 2019, India's smartphone market surpassed that of the United States.

158 million shipments were shipped, up 7% year over year. The market grew primarily as a result of Chinese brands' aggressive promotion and pricing. Despite the fact that China accounts for roughly 70% of global phone exports, India still has a 15% share, with Vietnam emerging as a key player with around 10% of such exports.

Digital India

Digital India may be a government of India initiative "designed to show India into a worldwide digitised hub" by revitalising the country's dormant digital business with the help of improved electronic communication, talent development, and different incentives to form the country technologically skeptical. It consists of diverse proposals and incentives offered to businesses, primarily domestic and international producing firms, to speculate in India and create the country a digital destination. The main target of the Digital India campaign is job creation and capability development in areas like Broadband Highways, e-Government, and Electronic Service Delivery, Universal Access to Mobile property, physics producing, and knowledge for All. The campaign's goal is to deal with accessibility challenges, permitting the USA to interact with each other and exchange awareness regarding problems and challenges that we tend to face. In sure cases, they conjointly provide near-real-time resolution of these issues. This project aims to assist India to improve the rural property by combining stable government policies with rewards and incentives provided through the campaign.

Simultaneously, the programme is meant to get jobs and improve capability growth, leading to an increase in gross domestic product and revenue.

Challenges in Implementation ofMake In India

The above-mentioned advantages of the Make in India concept would undoubtedly fuel our economic growth, and the current government's policies are praised around the globe. Although it is clear that countries and private sector players are excited about the concept and keen to invest in the manufacturing sector, the government must solve a few grey areas right away if the concept is to be applied seamlessly and efficiently. By other measures, India's labour laws are now out of date, making it almost difficult to hire, fire, or close down redundant businesses.

India has a federal structure in many respects, which restricts the central government's ability to enforce those schemes and principles. The state government's gambit involves providing utilities like electricity and water, as well as building facilities like highways, maintaining law and order, and allocating property. As a result, state government collaboration is critical for "Make in India."

Digital India

There is a major digital gap in India, which would be impossible to bridge in the four years reserved for the program.

Absence of a "Privacy Statute" and computer protection laws, the risk of human rights abuses, the lack of regulatory oversight of e-surveillance in India, the lack of intelligence reforms in India, and so on. Expose consumers to the risk of "identity theft," "domain abuse," and "cyberstalking" if they use these programs.

An e-governance program that does not provide process reengineering is yet another layer that provides no benefit. This will therefore limit opportunities for the vulnerable and oppressed.

The government must address the legitimate questions that have been raised. A "privacy law" and "data protection policies" are expected to improve people's confidence in such facilities. This would help to increase the efficiency of government services.

How Make in India and Digital India are progressing hand in hand

Since youth not only prefers to be self-employed but also prefers a quick life of which everyday transactions are a crucial feature, Digital India and Make in India are going hand in hand.

Furthermore, both campaigns work closely to help women entrepreneurs in the country on a variety of levels. Women are being empowered to move their companies forward with the help of benefits and services in both realms, allowing them to do so without having to deal with the hassles of collecting or paying payments.

“Today India is making considerable strides in the area of digital infrastructure,” Prime Minister Shri Narendra Modi said in an article in the Economic Times. In India, over 100 crore mobile phones are operational, and broadband connectivity is reaching villages. A GB of data costs less than a small bottle of iced tea. This data is now a service management tool.”

The government is aggressively encouraging digital payments, demonstrating that Digital India is evolving and allowing the country to savior and taste the flavor of online shopping even more than before.

"We're producing quality goods not just for India but for the world," PM Modi said in an Economic Times article about Make in India. India is establishing itself as a global powerhouse, especially in the fields of electronics and automotive manufacturing. We're on our way to becoming the world's leading manufacturer of smartphones."

Apart from digitizing physical stores/businesses, numerous online start-ups are essential for fostering digital payments in the region. In contrast, a safe, fast, and convenient digital payment mechanism is required for online start-ups to be effective.

The Indian digital payments market has come a long way from the days when online payment failure rates were as high as 40% and transactions took 60-80 seconds to complete. In contrast, the benefits of digital payments have now outweighed the disadvantages, and the bulk of the earlier bugs have been successfully overcome, allowing for the success in online transactions in the nation. As a result of technological advancements, completing each transaction now takes less than 10-15 seconds, according to the record.

With smartphones and broadband access touching every nook and cranny, the amount of transactions conducted via smartphones has risen dramatically.

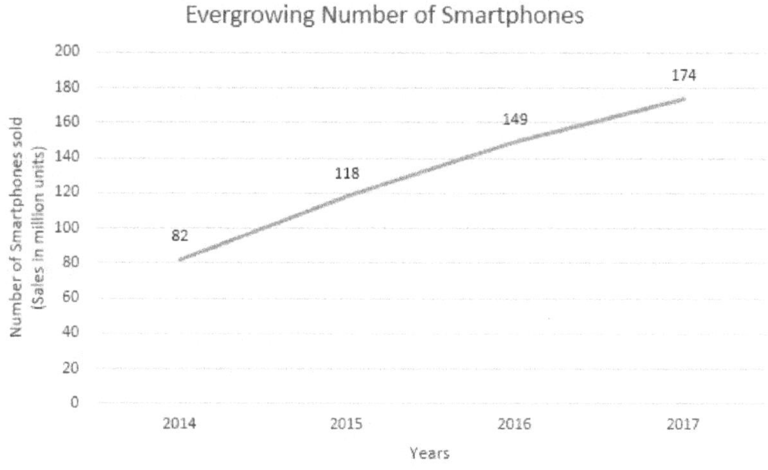

SOURCE: Lyra Network

The graph above shows the number of smartphones sold from 2014 to 2017.

Because of the increasing use of smartphones in the city, online transactions have increased from $86 million in 2011 to $1.15 billion in 2016.

With the growth in internet transactions all over the world, it's only normal that demand for online shopping has soared.

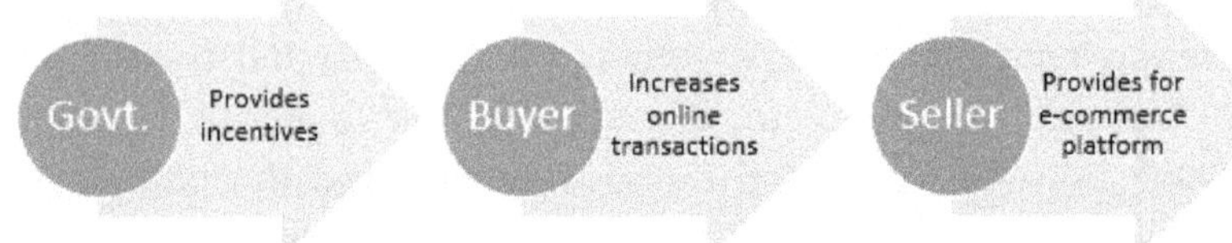

SOURCE: Lyra Network

Customers continue to shop digitally because the government has given numerous incentives to encourage the use of digital payments.

Customers benefit from these perks in addition to the other benefits of buying online, such as saving time, being more efficient than dealing with cash transfers, being cleaner, and being able to pay the same price without any hassle.

Since it lets the government keep track of each transaction, the government offers rewards and encourages online transactions. Which also helps to discourage tax avoidance and fraudulent transfers.

To overcome all of these obstacles, we must find some solutions –

1. A few new programs, particularly in electronics manufacturing and skill development, may be required.

2. Establish a dedicated training institute under DIP in each state to aid in increasing digital literacy and awareness.

3. To motivate young people to participate in effective DIP.

4. The government should hold seminars to educate people about digital services.

5. To publicize DIP policies in books, pen, TV, newspapers, and other media so that people are aware of the e-services.

6. Require a Digital India lecture in every educational institution to improve DIP policies.

7. To establish a DIP helpline number so that people can report problems with e-services.

8. Establish a help center in each state to address public issues.

9. To print e-Services booklets with images and distribute them to each home to raise awareness.

10. To transform villages into smart economic hubs that connect farmers directly to e-markets.

The crop's well-priced

Conclusion

The COVID-19 pandemic may present an opportunity, but structural reforms such as significant labour and land reforms, allowing businesses to hire and fire employees, handholding investors, direct tax benefits in SEZs, and plug-and-play facilities are required. India has the necessary manpower, but skill levels are lacking, and government regulations are relatively restrictive. This is an opportunity for India to expand its market access and assert itself as a global player. Finally, MAKE IN INDIA has resulted in a slew of new developments in a variety of fields. Furthermore, the pandemic's impact has altered the Indian economy's market structure.

Despite the fact that the digital India program is facing some challenges, it has a significant impact on India in terms of ensuring the best future for all citizens. We Indians, along with others, must collaborate to shape the knowledge economy. More job opportunities will become available to the nation's youth, boosting the economy. The Digital India campaign is a welcome step toward transforming India into a 21st-century powerhouse powered by connectivity and technological innovation.

This strategy is critical for eradicating India's unemployment and promoting growth. By addressing the problem of youth unemployment, we will significantly reduce poverty. The success of the Make in India initiative would undoubtedly propel the country's economy to new heights.

As a result, some social problems in the world could be resolved. The significance of these digitization efforts is that they will result in planned economic and societal growth as a result of the widespread adoption of digital technologies.

References

- "Focus on 'Make In India'". Business Standard. 25 September 2014. Retrieved27 February 2015.
- "Look East, Link West, says PM Modi at Make in India launch". Hindustan Times. 25 September 2014. Retrieved 27 February 2015.
- Kamal, N. (2017). Impact of „Make in India" on Automobile Sector. International Journal of Business Administration and Management, 74-89.
- Raj, K., & Aithal, P. S. (2018). Digitization of India-Impact on the BOP Sector. International Journal of Management, Technology, and Social Sciences (IJMTS), 3(1), 59-74.
- Midha, R. (2016, August). Digital India: barriers & remedies. In International Conference on Recent Innovations in Sciences, Management, Education and Technology (pp. 256-261).
- Kedar, M. S. (2015). Digital India new way of innovating India digitally. International Research Journal of Multidisciplinary Studies, 1(4), 34-49.
- https://www.sscadda.com/make-in-india#:~:text=To%20erode%20unemployment%20from%20India,
- of%20Make%20in%20India%20campaign.
- https://inc42.com/features/startupindia-how-digital
- -india-and-make-in-india-power-indias-tech-juggernaut/#:~:text=While%20Make%20In%20India%2
- 0was,education%20to%20commerce%20and%20governance.
- https://www.lyra.com/in/make-in-india-and-digital-india/
- https://www.digitalindia.gov.in/
- http://www.businessworld.in/article/Digital-Manufacturing-The-New-Goal-for-Digital-India-Make-in-India-and-Start-up-India/12-03-2021-383679/
- http://www.makeinindia.com/
- https://en.wikipedia.org/wiki/Digital_India
- https://byjus.com/free-ias-prep/digital-india/

List Of Authors

1. A study on the Impact on Self Help Groups during and Post Covid 19

- **Mr. Sajith Kumar B,** Head Of the Department, People Institute Of Management, Studies, Munnad, Kannur University, Kerala.
- **Prof. Thimmaiah Bayavanda Chinnappa** - Moskovskaya Shkoloo Upraveleniya, Scolkovo, Novaya Ulitsa, 100, Scolkovo , Moscow Oblast, Russia.
- **Mrs. Sajina T Mohan,** Assistant Professor, Sanatana Arts And Science College, Mavungal, Kasaragod, Kannur University, Kerala.

2. Use of Social Media: An Innovation during the Covid 19

- **Krittibas Datta,** State Aided College Teacher, Department of Political Science, Jalangi Mahavidyalaya, Jalangi, Murshidabad, West Bengal.

3. An analysis of the "Make in India" program and its prospect

- **Satish Kumar Gupta,** Assistant Professor Gopal Narayan Singh University
- **Dr.Sandeep Kumar Kesarwani,** Associate Professor Gopal Narayan Singh University

4. Outcomes of COVID 19 featured by students of School Education System in Punjab province

- **Ms.KinzaHafeez,** Punjab School Education Dept. Punjab
- **Dr. Saira Taiba,** Research Scholar Islamic research center, Department of Islamic Studies, B.Z.U. Multan, Pakistan
- **Dr.Tariq Mehmood,** Punjab school Education Dept., Punjab
- **Furqan Majeed,** Punjab School Education Dept. Punjab

5. Online Teacher Education Programme For Higher Education School System To Present Situation Of Covid-19 Pandemic Period

- **Rajarshi Roy Chowdhury,** B.Ed 4th semester student, Sagarpara Education college, Sagarpara, Murshidabad
- **Mallika Mondal,** B.Ed 4th semester student, M. R B.Ed. College, West Bengal.

6.Covid-19 Vaccination Drive in India: Facilitation to Front Doorstep

- **Dr. Abhishek Srivastava,** *Associate Professor,* Faculty of Management Studies, Gopal Narayan Singh University, Rohtas

7. Changing Attitudes Among Teenagers During And After Covid-19: An Analytical Study

- ***Prashanth Kumar HP,*** Assistant Professor, Dept of Biotechnology, B.M.S College of Engineering, Bull Temple Rd, Basavanagudi, Bengaluru, Karnataka 560019.
- **P. Horsley Solomon**, Head, Department of Electronics Science, SRM Arts and Science College, Kattankulathur - 603 203, Chengalpattu Dist.
- **Sayan Chakraborty**, International Author, and Motivational Speaker.

8.“2020:Covid–19 Hits The Education System”

- **Pradip Das,** M.A.M.Ed.,Ph. D-Scholar-, OPJS University, Churu, Rajasthan.

9.COVID-19 Vaccine Diplomacy in the Indo-Pacific Region

- **Mr. UdayModak,** Assistant Professor, Bhavan's Tripura College of Teacher Education (BTCTE), Bimangarh, Narasingarh, Agartala, Tripura

10. School Students Academic Stress And Anxiety In The Covid-19 Vaccination

- **Dr. Kotra Balayogi,** Assistant Professor, Unity College of Teacher Education, Dimapur, Nagaland.

11. Post-Covid Challenges And Coping Strategies For Retail Industry In India: An Empirical Study

- **Dr.V.P.Sriram**, Professor, Department of MBA, Acharya Bangalore B School (ABBS), Bengaluru, Karnataka, India.
- **Prof. (Dr) Aruna Anchal**Dean & Head, Dept. of Education, Baba Mast Nath University, Asthal Bohar, Rohtak, Haryana 124021.

12. Innovation In Response To The Covid-19 Crisis

- **Dr. Savita Mishra**, Principal, Vidyasagar College of Education, Phansidewa, Darjeeling, West Bengal.

- **Kanishka,** Pupil Teacher, Manvi Institute of Education and Technology, SCERT, New Delhi.
- **Dr. Anshika Rajvanshi,** Sr. Assistant Professor, IIMT, Delhi.

13.Covid-19 Variants: Alpha Beta Delta And Omicron

- **Jakir Ali Kazi**, Independent Scholar, M.A in Political Science, Department of Political Science, University of Gour Banga, Malda, West Bengal.

14. Covid Vaccine Plan Of India

- **Dr. Ekata Gupta**, Associate Professor,Guru Nanak Institute of Management, Delhi.
- **Divine Tomar**, Pupil-Teacher, Manvi Institute Of Education & Technology, SCERT, New Delhi.
- **Nilesh Kumar Dokania**, Assistant Professor,Guru Nanak Institute of Management, Delhi.

15. New Way of Innovating India Digitally: "Make In India" During Covid 19

- **Dr. Mukta Goyal,** Principal, Manvi Institute of Education & Technology, SCERT, New Delhi.

www.ingramcontent.com/pod-product-compliance
Ingram Content Group UK Ltd.
Pitfield, Milton Keynes, MK11 3LW, UK
UKHW021911190726
13853UKWH00002B/624

9 798886 060126